THE GOLDEN BOOK
OF THE
MYSTERIOUS

THE GOLDEN BOOK
OF THE
MYSTERIOUS

by Jane Werner Watson and Sol Chaneles
Illustrations by Alan Lee

GOLDEN PRESS · NEW YORK
WESTERN PUBLISHING COMPANY, INC., RACINE, WISCONSIN

An original work created by
Vineyard Books, Inc.
159 East 64th Street
New York, N.Y. 10021

Copyright © 1976 by Western Publishing Company, Inc.
All Rights Reserved
Printed in the U.S.A.
Golden, A Golden Book® and Golden Press® are trademarks of
Western Publishing Company, Inc.
Library of Congress Catalog Card Number: 75-42989

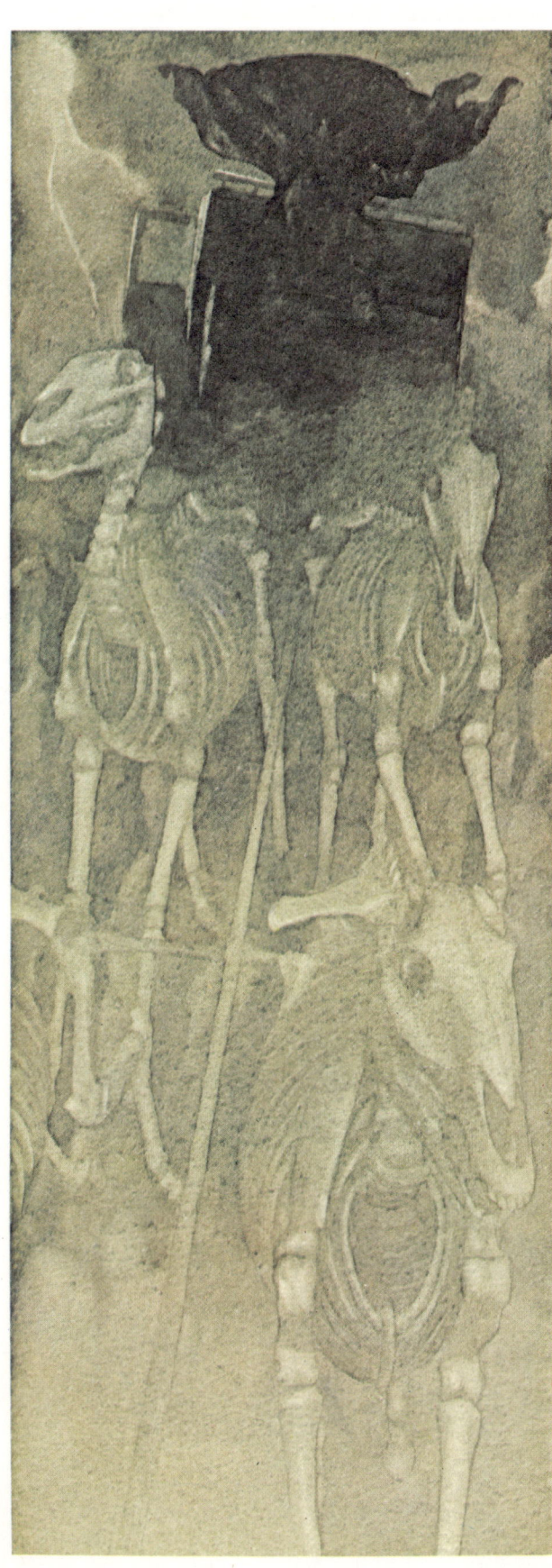

CONTENTS

INTRODUCTION 7

CREATURES OF MYSTERY
Monsters of the Deep 11 · The Marvelous Unicorn 13 · Yeti and Susquatch, Creatures of the Wilds 15 · Werewolves and Vampires by Moonlight 18 · Sirens and Mermaids 21 · The Loch Ness Monster 24

MYSTERIOUS POWERS OF MIND AND SPIRIT
Hypnosis 26 · Thought Transfer 31 · Mysterious Sights and Sounds 36 · Contacts with Spirits 39 · Eastern Psychic Wisdom 40 · Ouija and Automatic Writing 46 · Ghostly Apparitions and Poltergeists 49 · Travel Outside the Body 53 · Levitation 56 · Foreknowledge 58 · Reincarnation: Have You Lived Before? 60

MYSTERIES SCIENCE CAN'T EXPLAIN
Seeing Through the Skin 66 · Hibernation: Possibilities for Space Travel 68 · Dowsing: Strange Power in the Hands 70 · Rainmaking 72 · Auras of Many Colors 74 · The Homing Instinct 77 · Do Plants Have Feelings? 79 · Snake Charmers 83 · The Power to Heal 85 · Strange Flames 90 · Unidentified Flying Objects 91

WITCHCRAFT, SORCERY AND THE OCCULT
What Is Witchcraft? 100 · Sorcery and Spells 107 · Alchemy 110 · Fortunetelling 113

MYSTERIOUS DISAPPEARANCES
Ships Without Crews 126 · Lost Settlements 129 · Lost Civilizations 130 · Vanished Peoples of the Past 133

EPILOGUE 140

INDEX 141

*The most beautiful thing
we can experience is the mysterious.
It is the source of all true art
and science.*
—ALBERT EINSTEIN,
"What I Believe,"
in Forum, October 1930

INTRODUCTION

WHAT IS A MYSTERY?

A mystery, according to a dictionary, may be any fact, matter or phenomenon of which the meaning, cause or explanation is unknown and which arouses curiosity or inspires awe.

Without curiosity and awe—the desire to learn about something strange or unknown combined with reverence and a tinge of fear—mankind would never have come down from the trees or out of the cave. In fact he never would have developed any civilization at all.

It has been man's endless quest for understanding the mysteries of life that has led to all learning and culture. Awestruck before the power of the forces of nature—of sun, rain, storm and self-renewing life—mankind developed religion. Inspired by a sense of wonder at the mysteries of the cosmos (including those of the human heart), mankind created most of the world's great art and poetry.

Curiosity about the mysterious workings of life in all its myriad forms has also led to the development of science and technology. Indeed it would be valid to say that fascination with mystery is one of the most basic and priceless qualities of human nature.

"But all the big mysteries have been solved," you may sigh. "Man has walked on the moon, listened to the music of the stars, peered out to the frontiers of the universe, split the heart of the atom, harnessed the fearsome energy of the sun itself. What is left for us to marvel and wonder at?"

Fear not, reader! The world is still full of tantalizing and intriguing mysteries. In the pages that follow you will be briefly introduced to a vast range of mysterious matters great and small that still pique human curiosity. Many of them are at this moment leading human thinking toward new horizons.

Some of these unknowns lead us back into the hazy, scantly understood eras of pre-history. Others lure us into long-forsaken caverns and nameless tombs, down to unexplored depths of the seas, out into possibly inhabited reaches of space. Still other mysteries—including some of the most challenging and fascinating—lead us to look into our own minds and hearts and spirits, even at our own familiar fingertips, with fresh awareness and heightened sensitivity. That, after all, is the magic of mystery—its power to open our eyes and minds, to stimulate our boundless curiosity.

Will we find any of the answers? Possibly. But it is the pursuit, not the conquest, that provides the thrill. In the words of an old saying, "The end is nothing; the road is all." So, as you embark on this journey of exploration down strange and wondrous, often shadowy roads, we wish you well. Open your mind, indulge your imagination and enjoy the mysteries of the world!

CREATURES OF MYSTERY

Thus the sum of things is ever being renewed, and mortals live dependent one upon another. Some races increase, others diminish, and in a short space the generations of living creatures are changed and like runners hand on the torch of life.

—LUCRETIUS, De Rerum Natura

Monsters of the Deep

Maps of the world drawn in the sixteenth century often show monsters rearing up from the Atlantic and Pacific oceans. They may have huge, craggy heads and fangs jutting from their gaping jaws. Some are shown thrashing the waves with forked and flailing tails, while others rise above the surface on wide-jutting wings.

A few of the pictured monsters resemble the whales with which we are more or less familiar, and those we can accept. At the rest we are likely to smile and shake our heads. How ignorant and superstitious those old seamen were! we think to ourselves.

We feel superior to the sailors who were terrified at the prospect of sailing out onto Ocean Deep for fear they might fall off the edge of the flat world or be swallowed by the monsters thought to live in those dreaded waters. We know the world is round, not flat—though few of us could have figured it out for ourselves. And we feel just as confident that the oldsters were wrong about the existence of sea monsters. But were they?

There are certainly whales as much as 100 feet long that can smash a boat to splinters with one flip of their tails. Many of them have been harpooned, so their existence cannot be denied. We know of giant squid with arm spreads of eighty feet. Men have killed some of those in recent years, so we believe in them, though for many years they too were thought to be figments of fevered imaginations. Why should we not believe in those monsters that thus far have succeeded in getting away?

Sea serpents forty-five to eighty feet long, writhing along with their bodies looped in huge coils, have been reported in the Atlantic by respected naval officers. The head of one, held high above the waves where it could be clearly seen, was described as being about six feet long.

It is true that no such monster has ever been netted or harpooned. But skeletons have been found of huge, long-necked sea serpents that lived 100 million years ago. They are called plesiosaurs and elasmosaurs.

Could any family live for 100 million years? Well, dinosaurs small and large lasted longer than that. Cockroaches and some other insects have existed several times that long. In 1938 a strange fish called a coelacanth was caught off Africa. It is known from fossils that this family lived 350 million years ago. Like the dinosaurs and plesiosaurs, it was thought to have vanished from the earth. But evidently it had just retreated to the ocean depths, where it grows to be as much as five feet long today. Isn't it possible that some families of sea serpents have lived in those depths to this very day?

Certainly whole groups of sober men have described long, serpentlike sea creatures of great size. Those who saw one said that it had a head like a ten-gallon barrel, with round, red, flashing eyes and a finlike mane spreading out along its neck.

Carved likenesses of sea serpents have been found that date from about A.D. 230 and 1000, and tales in which they appear date back hundreds of years earlier still. Some of these reports did become twisted and enlarged as they were passed along. We might think of them as fanciful make-believe but for the fact that people continue to report seeing sea serpents.

As recently as 1948, 1950 and 1970 a number of sightings were reported. And several times, from Florida, Cuba and South Africa, came reports that huge, deep, three-toed footprints had been found, some in sand so hard that a 200-pound man scarcely left a trace as he walked across it.

Still, the mysterious sea serpents manage to evade deep-sea fishermen. Nor has anyone with a camera managed to snap one of these reported beasts paddling along, with its relatively small head lifted high out of the water on a long swaying neck. Maybe some day proof will come that these creatures out of ancient times really do swim the seas.

The Marvelous Unicorn

Across the pages of ancient writers, as much as 2,000 years ago, bounded the swift, elusive figure of the unicorn. With the body and head of a sleek white horse, the swift hind legs of an antelope, the tail of a lion and the beard of a goat, the unicorn's principal claim to fame was the long, sharp, twisted horn that rose from its forehead and tapered to a point at a length of 24 to 36 inches.

Early reports of unicorns located them in India and made them sound much like wild asses or the oryx, which is a swift and long-horned antelope. The oryx has two horns, but these are so straight that, seen from the side and for a brief moment, they could easily appear to be one.

As travelers from the West became more familiar with India, it became clear that the unicorn was not to be found there. But people would not give up the dream of finding it, so storytellers relocated it in Africa, where it has been reported in recent times. In the early 1800s a South African farmer described an animal that was shot near his home as having yellow and black stripes and a "hard, bony substance covered with hair and ten feet long" protruding from the middle of its forehead.

A missionary stationed in Africa heard tales from the local inhabitants of a fierce and dangerous one-horned animal that sounded like a unicorn. Rumors of "horses with one horn" kept cropping up as recently as a hundred years or so ago.

Not all of the sightings were associated with India and Africa. Chinese literature speaks of animals known as the "four-not-likes"—because while they had attributes of the horse, the antelope, the goat and the lion, they were none of these.

Though the unicorn had been mentioned in literature repeatedly since the times of ancient Greece and Rome—and some scholars even thought they had found references to it in the Hebrew text of the Old Testament—this exotic animal reached the peak of its fame in the Middle Ages.

During the fifteenth century the unicorn became associated with noble families and soon won a place on the royal arms of Scotland, with a crown about its neck and often with another on its head.

Marvelous powers were credited to the unicorn, powers centering about its wonderful horn, which was often described as being white at the base, black at the middle and red at the tip. It was widely believed that in the wild a unicorn could instantly turn the water from a woodland pool crystal clear, sweet and pure by touching its horn to the water while drinking.

Powdered horn was used as an ingredient in medicines prescribed against plague. And a potion made of heated and ground horn was considered a powerful antidote to poisons.

At the court of France, as late as 1789, the year of the French Revolution, it was still a part of ceremonial ritual to test the king's food for poison with bowls or implements presumably made from unicorn horns. These were said to react to any trace of poison.

This practice, since it was rather widespread in historic times, would seem to have had some basis in reality. There must have been some regular source of horns recognizable as having come from the foreheads of these marvelous beasts.

One possible way to get a horn was, of course, to go into the forest and catch a unicorn. This was no mean feat, since the beast was purported to be not only the swiftest of animals but also fierce enough to attack and best an elephant.

One ancient source reported that this savage and quarrelsome nature was softened to milk-mildness by the approach of the mating season and that the unicorn was very gentle with its mate. The Christian Church in medieval times used the unicorn as a symbol of purity and the power of love, associating the swift and mighty beast with the lamb and dove. And the belief spread that the unicorn could be subdued without effort by a pure maiden. At the sight of one, it was said, the elusive beast would come and place its head submissively in her lap.

There is no record as to how many unicorns were actually captured by maidens of spotless purity in order that the magic power of their horns might be utilized. Some skeptics believe that other creatures were willfully or otherwise confused with unicorns.

The only one-horned animals known positively are the rhinoceros and the narwhal, or narwhale, a relatively small, pale-skinned arctic whale. It is difficult to imagine the tales of speed and grace associated with the unicorn having had their origin in the squat and clumsy bulk of the rhinoceros, with its stubby, curved horn. Whaling, however, was for many centuries a lively industry. And almost certainly some sailors did display and offer for sale as unicorn horns the ivory tusks of narwhals.

Another possible explanation is the legend claiming that the unicorn was thrown out of Noah's ark and drowned, and so its kind vanished from the earth.

Yeti and Susquatch, Creatures of the Wilds

If you trek through the remote mountains of the Himalayas you may hear a strange, half-human call, part yelp, part meow. You may see strange figures shambling across a snowfield in the distance. But as you draw near, they will have vanished, leaving only footprints in the snow.

Unless you are much luckier than most—if you want to call it luck—that is as much as you can hope to see of the strange creatures known to the mountain people as yeti and to many outsiders as Abominable Snowmen.

The footprints that have been found have varied in size; the small prints may belong to youngsters, it is thought. Some have had four toes, others five. The distance between prints has been twice as long as the stride of an average man. This suggests, as some who have glimpsed them have claimed, that yeti may be as much as ten feet tall. And they move across the ice and snow three times as fast as the speediest mountaineer.

Eyewitnesses describe the strange beings as shaggy but with hairless faces. Some say their heads are shaped like squares; some report high domes. They have been seen at ranges as close as twenty-five feet but never by a man with a camera at the ready, though several expeditions have searched the mountain ranges for a trace of them.

Once it seemed that the mystery was about to be solved. That was back in 1902, when a British construction crew was at work in the Himalayas. One day some workers were missing from camp, so part of the crew went out to look for them. In their search they came upon a manlike creature with a bare face, large yellow fangs and a furry body. Fearing for their safety, the searchers shot the creature dead. But before measurements could be taken and a study made, the body mysteriously disappeared.

In 1913 a group of Chinese hunters in Sinkiang, north of the Himalayas, captured a manlike creature alive. They said he had powerful hands and feet like those of a man rather than an ape. His face was dark, his hairy coat silvery yellow. He made various sounds that his captors could not understand, though there may have been an effort to communicate. After a few months, regrettably, the mysterious captive fell ill and died.

In 1955 a French expedition found 3,000 separate footprints in new-fallen Himalayan snow. Those footprints did not match the paw marks of any known animals of the region—wolves, foxes, snow leopards. They were more apelike. And indeed the yeti does nearly fit the description of a giant ape in color, size, footprints and length of stride.

An American trekking through the Himalayas in 1963 came upon what he believed was a yeti den. It was a cave containing a bed of juniper branches that could have been torn off only by a creature of mighty strength. There was some red-brown hair caught in the branches, and there were both food scraps and droppings in the cave. It was recalled that the African gorilla also makes a bed—in his case, of bamboo.

Hundreds of people far to the northeast of the Himalayas, in Outer Mongolia, have also reported seeing a terrifying and remarkable creature that walked on two feet.

In 1964 two humanlike skulls were unearthed there. Since no skeletons have been found above ground, some people think that the yeti must bury their dead. But what tools would they use to dig into the frozen ground of the mountain regions where they live? Tibetans, because of the hardness of the ground and the shortage of fuel for cremation, dismember their corpses and leave them to vultures and wild animals.

Some people wonder whether the yeti may actually be pre-human beings left over from the distant past. They may have become isolated during the last Ice Age, the theory goes. Instead of rejoining humankind in a move to milder climates, they have, for an unknown reason, remained in this land of inhospitable rock and year-round snows. Since the country offers few opportunities for broader lives or for learning new skills, the yeti have remained primitive, though they have been reported as having sharp eyes and large brain capacity.

The high Himalayas are not the only region where mysterious creatures of this sort have been seen in recent times. Over the past 100 years numerous sightings have also been reported in the mountains near the Pacific Ocean from California to British Columbia and in Montana.

Susquatch, or Bigfoot, as the North American species of the monster is often called, must weigh 1,000 pounds and be about six feet, ten inches tall, judging from his tracks. He seems to be both quick-witted and helpful. Not long ago a man pinned under his car after a mountain accident was freed by a powerful creature that carried him to the nearest habitation, then vanished silently.

In 1967 a film was shot of Bigfoot. It was blurred, but the manlike form that can be seen in it matches many descriptions provided by reputable people.

As recently as, the autumn of 1973 three fishermen near Vancouver saw a figure about ten feet tall and lightish gray in tone walking slowly along the beach. So Bigfoot is alive and well, it seems, in the Pacific Northwest. And in 1958 an American scientist reported from the Himalayas that he was convinced there were yeti—low-grade human or subhuman creatures who lived without fire—making their homes there in remote mountain caves.

Stranger still are reports of appearances of mysterious and gigantic creatures in inhabited areas. In 1973, near a small Illinois town, a creature was repeatedly reported, variously described as seven to eight feet tall, pale in color, shaggy-haired, matted with mud and smelling of river slime.

Sheriff's deputies investigating several reports found trails of slime near the spots where the "thing" had been seen and peculiar footprints on the banks of the Big Muddy River. They heard weird cries. Their dogs picked up a strange scent and at one point retreated from the search, whining. But they did not find the monster. They filed an "unknown creature" report, and there the matter rests.

Werewolves and Vampires by Moonlight

A full moon shines coldly down on the sleeping countryside. Suddenly from the deep shadows comes a ghastly howl. It may be a dog out on the prowl, responding as dogs do to the eerie light. In some areas it may be a coyote or a jackal. But beware, say many people; it may be a werewolf—or, depending on the part of the world in which you hear the haunting cry, a tiger, lion, leopard or boar—containing a tortured human soul.

A werewolf is the animal form into which a troubled man or woman may secretly change —or so it is said—by the light of the moon. After a bloodthirsty outing under cover of darkness, the werewolf—or other animal—generally can regain its human form.

In its animal form a werewolf is said to be much like other wolves but unusually large, fierce and both hungry and thirsty to extremes. It has dry eyes, very long, pointed front teeth and lacks a tail. In human form a werewolf usually has slanting eyebrows that meet in a sharp V over the bridge of its nose. He has an unusually long middle finger on each hand and long, curling reddish fingernails. His body is unusually hairy, particularly on the hands and feet.

Sometimes the transition is not complete. The werewolf may have a human face and a wolf's body, or vice versa. Usually it walks with a stumbling gait.

Tales of human beings who take on animal form for cannibalistic ventures have been common around the world—from Europe to India and the Far East, from tropical Africa and Central America to the Arctic. Usually they are said to dote on the flesh and blood of young girls.

In the Middle Ages, when witchcraft and various forms of enchantment and possession were accepted as matter-of-fact truths, scores of werewolves confessed to their crimes or were tried and convicted and burned at the stake.

One sixteenth-century werewolf whose human name was Peter Stubbs was said to have murdered and devoured victims for twenty-five years without being discovered before he fled as a wolf and regained his human form within sight of his pursuers. He was then clubbed to death. At least one other werewolf of the same period was buried alive for his revolting crimes.

Thousands of eyewitness reports dating from ancient times up into the twentieth century suggest that there may be something more than fearful moonlit fantasy behind these horrid tales.

One theory is that the afflicted people suffer from a mental disease called lycanthropy. Its victims believe that they are wild animals. They may howl, eat raw meat and run around on all fours. But this theory scarcely accounts for their looking like wolves to unaffected people.

Another explanation offered is that werewolves may be victims of a rare disease—hypertrichosis or perhaps porphyria. Hypertrichosis causes an unusually heavy growth of hair on all parts of the body and face.

Those who suffer from porphyria usually are hairy, too, and have reddish teeth. They are often mentally disturbed, and their eyes are so hypersensitive to light that they prefer being active only at night.

One expert, a trained biologist, reported in recent years having seen some teenage victims of a related disease in the remote mountains of Norway. They had hairy bodies, protruding jaws and short, bowed legs, and they were mentally retarded. The scientist blamed their condition on severe vitamin deficiencies caused in part by the dank, sunless climate.

More fanciful causes for werewolves have been listed. These include eating the brain of a wolf or drinking from the pawprint of a wolf. Even drinking by chance from a pool whose waters wolves have lapped can lead, it has been rumored, to a transformation.

Other interested people insist, however, that werewolves have sold their souls to the devil in a special, complicated ceremony. On a night with a full moon a person wishing to make this fiendish pact must go to the crest of a hill and there bathe naked in the moonlight.

He must draw two circles on the ground, an inner circle three feet in diameter and an outer one of seven feet. At midnight a fire must be lighted under a big black cauldron in the center of the inner circle.

In the cauldron a true witch's brew, in a special combination, must be boiled, consisting of henbane, opium, hemlock, the fat of young children, cowbine, sweet flag, cinquefoil, bats' blood and belladonna. After incantations have been chanted over the bubbling mixture, it must be smeared all over one's naked body. While this is done, various chants must be repeated, chants such as this: "Make me a werewolf! Make me a man-eater! Make me a werewolf! Make me a woman-eater! Make me a werewolf! Make me a child-eater! I pine for blood! Human blood! Give it me! Give it me tonight! Great wolf spirit, give it me, and, heart, body and soul, I am yours!"

Why anyone should wish voluntarily to enter into this terrible pact is never explained. Modern instances of vampirism, a condition marked by an uncontrollable longing for human blood, have been documented, however.

In one instance a young girl was on the beach with a young man who, while swimming, scraped his shoulder raw on a rock. The girl stared with wild fascination at the blood oozing from the wound. Suddenly she bent forward and sucked greedily at the blood. The young man soon learned that she was dying of leukemia, which was destroying her own red blood cells. Perhaps the disease was responsible for her blood lust.

Some years ago in the Midwest a young man committed several grisly murders for the purpose of procuring fresh blood to drink. It was assumed that he was insane.

Whatever the cause, lycanthropy and vampirism, wrapped in terrible mystery, cannot easily be shrugged off as mere figments of an active imagination.

Sirens and Mermaids

As Odysseus made his way home from the Trojan War, the gentle breeze that sped his ship along gave way one day to a breathless calm. Then Odysseus saw, seated on the shore, the Sirens—those sisters with the soft bodies of birds and the faces of beautiful women who lured men to their death with their enchanting singing.

Fortunately Odysseus had been well warned, so he stuffed plugs of wax into the ears of his oarsmen and made them tie him to the mast. Thus protected, they rowed stoutly on their way, while Odysseus listened to the Sirens' haunting song. Like all the others whose bones were whitening on the rocks, he pleaded with his men to turn aside so that he might hear more. Only because they could not hear either his pleas or the Sirens' songs, the ship was saved that day. So goes one of the most famous early stories of sea sirens, from Homer's *Odyssey*.

Many other sailors down through the centuries have reported being lured to keel-smashing rocks by the songs of lovely maidens. On the Rhine River it was Lorelei who crooned to the sailors as she combed her golden hair with a comb of gold.

What lay behind these legends of the sirens and their fatal songs? Was it the wailing of the wind above the moaning and sighing of rock-tossed waters? Or did the sailors who survived shipwrecks fabricate the tales as a romantic excuse for their catastrophes?

The widespread tales of siren songs are one of the mysteries of the seas. Mermaids are another.

Mermaids resembled sirens in some of the tales that were told. They were often described as lovely creatures—beautiful young women from the waist up, fishlike from the waist down. In some stories they were seated on rocks or floating on the surface of the water, combing their long hair as they peered happily into hand mirrors. When they were attracted to a sailor, they used their beauty and their wiles to lure him down to their undersea home. These mermaids are known as daughters of the King of the Sea.

That is the fairytale aspect of mermaids, who are presumed to have the power to see the future and to perform certain enchantments. There have, however, been many more matter-of-fact accounts of sightings of mermaids which suggest that, as with many legends, there is behind them a framework of truth.

Some unromantic souls relate sailors' reports of mermaids to sea cows. These mammals, called the dugong and the manatee, live in warm Atlantic waters and lift their heads above the waves to nurse their young. They are blunt-faced, bulky creatures, ten feet long, with steel-gray hides and paddle-shaped "arms." A sailor would have to be really lonely and to have been at sea a long, long time to see feminine beauty in a manatee!

In the early days of transatlantic trade and whaling trips to the South Seas, crews were away from their home port months or even years at a time. But there is a more attractive alternate explanation available. The mermaids were probably really seals.

Seals are graceful and appealing creatures, and they assume almost human poses as they loll in the sun on rocks. Their round heads, even the extremely mobile flippers with which they rub their bodies, might well appear semihuman at a distance, with the dazzling sun on the water blurring the sight. And the call of the seals, while it sounds like a bark to many, can have a haunting musical quality. Most seals are dull gray, but in 1956 a zoologist discovered a female seal of an unusual salmon-pink tone that, to a lonely sailor, might well suggest a mermaid's rosy blush.

Even this explanation, though, does not account for some of the sightings matter-of-factly reported. One of the most striking took place in 1830 in the Hebrides, a group of islands off the western coast of Scotland. Many of the islanders were working at the shore when one of them spotted a "woman in miniature" cavorting in the sea. The whole group watched her play about until a thoughtless boy threw a stone which struck her.

She vanished from sight, and a few days later her dead body was washed ashore. The upper part of her body resembled that of a well-developed child, with long, glossy hair and soft skin. The lower part was like a salmon, smooth and scaleless. The sheriff of the district had the body buried in a coffin, near the shore.

Another dead mermaid was reported taken aboard by a freighter bound from Panama to New Orleans back in 1881. The ship's log records that she was a female human being to the waist, with head, arms and body, though her hair was like seaweed and her fingers were claws. From the waist down, though, she was a manatee or sea cow.

That was a semitropical sighting, but most of the rest of the sightings reported have been in or near Scotland, strangely.

One Scotsman out walking his dog on a sandy beach claimed to have come upon a mermaid seated on a rock that had been submerged at high tide not long before. Her red-brown hair was still dripping wet, and her fish tail glistened

damply. She seemed to be waiting for the tide to come in again to float her out to sea.

When she saw that she was being observed, the mermaid turned away, rolled down the rock, humped clumsily across the beach on her fish tail and vanished in the surf.

There were other sightings in the same area, one by a married couple out fishing in a small boat. They were startled to see a pretty, green-eyed face peering out from a tangle of floating seaweed. But on meeting their gaze, she too vanished from sight.

Another mermaid—or merman, for the old tales mention both sexes—was encountered in 1957 in the Pacific. A sailor crossing the ocean by raft, Tahiti-bound, reported that he was knocked down one night by a creature that pulled itself aboard, stood upright on its tail and then flung itself upon him.

The hair of the merman's head was like seaweed, he said, its face human but rather coarse. Where the creature had struck him the sailor later found a few fishlike scales caught in his clothing. When he reached shore he showed these to an ichthyologist (an expert on fish), who told him that they had come from no known sea animal. How unfortunate it was that no one else was on hand to share and verify this experience!

The Loch Ness Monster

Not all monsters live in the oceans. The most famous of all is located in a Scottish lake, or loch, one of many that were cut off from the sea by rising land within the past several thousand years. Loch Ness, the home of Nessie—as the monster is called—is a deep, rough-bottomed lake with a wildly beautiful shoreline. It is by no means a wilderness area, though, for its northern end approaches the city of Inverness. Many people use the loch for recreation, and a good number of them have reported seeing Nessie.

Radio, a submarine and powerful cameras have been put to work in search of the monster. But the only solid result to date has been one shadowy photograph taken on a misty morning from a distance of several miles. All that can be seen is an outline of a small head poised on a long, curving neck—much as many of the sighters of sea serpents have reported.

One young oceanographer who pursued Nessie by submarine got soundings that indicated he was getting close. But Nessie was much swifter than the small submarine and succeeded in getting away.

Other lake-dwelling monsters have been seen in nearby Loch Morer, on the shores of Irish lakes and at sites in Canada. There seems no reason not to take these reports seriously.

MYSTERIOUS POWERS OF MIND AND SPIRIT

Mysterious messages, midnight seances, travel outside the body, tables that tap out words, ghosts that bang windows—these may sound like raw materials for an eerie movie thriller. But many intelligent, down-to-earth people claim to have had contact with spirits or other experiences with supernatural powers. Such numerous and often well-documented claims warrant a close look at some of the phenomena involved.

Hypnosis

"Watch this small ball swinging gently on its chain," says the hypnotist. "It swings slowly, slowly. Count to yourself as it swings. As you count, you will relax. Your body will feel very heavy. Before you reach one hundred, you will be completely relaxed."

The subject watches the ball and counts slowly, evenly. Soon the counting can no longer be heard. The subject is completely relaxed—or hypnotized.

"Now hold out your right hand," says the hypnotist. The subject does, though he (or she) does not seem to be listening. "I will prick your fingers with this pin," says the hypnotist, "but you will not feel any pain." He jabs the sharp pin firmly into the tip of each finger in turn. The subject feels nothing.

This is just one example of the power of hypnosis—to free a person from pain. Doctors sometimes use this power to make patients comfortable, though their illness or injury may cause them great pain normally.

A hypnotic trance may be shallow, so that the subject has his eyes open and seems close to being awake. It may be deep, like the trance of someone who walks in his sleep. When the hypnotist says, "Now you are going to wake up," or something of the sort, to end the trance, the subject will have no memory of what went on in the trance. But he may still follow suggestions the hypnotist made during it.

"When you wake up, your headache will be gone," the hypnotist may say to someone suffering from a severe headache. "You will be so happy that you will do a little dance."

On awakening, the subject will say, "I feel so rested. My headache has cleared up entirely. What a relief!" And rising from the chair, he or she does a happy little dance step, with no thought of having been told to do this.

Hypnosis can also help people overcome personal habits that they dislike but cannot change unaided. "When you wake up you will not like cigarettes any more," the hypnotist may say. Or "You will no longer have a longing for sweets." This kind of instruction, known as post-hypnotic suggestion, can help people give up smoking or overeating.

Making use of a swinging ball or a pocket watch is just one example of the possible ways to hypnotize a subject. Proper use of hypnosis takes training. Many different methods can be used, depending on the subject and the situation. The hypnotist may speak in a slow, rhythmic voice, repeating a message or instruction monotonously. He may stroke the subject's forehead gently, saying, "Now you will feel very sleepy," or something of the sort.

When the subject is in a hypnotic trance he will follow instructions from the hypnotist—as long as he is not asked to do anything he would refuse to do when awake.

Hypnosis as Therapy

Doctors may use hypnosis to release tensions in muscles—or in the mind. Not only can the pain of dentistry, surgery, childbirth or serious illness be greatly reduced. Many physical conditions that are caused by stress, tension or pressure can also be relieved by relaxation under hypnosis. Among these are high blood pressure, asthma, disorders of the digestive tract, skin problems and migraine headaches.

People who have been depressed can through hypnosis be made more cheerful and confident that they will get better. Will power can be strengthened by suggestions made under hypnosis—for example to help people who have difficulty studying, giving up smoking or nail biting or sticking to a diet or exercise program.

Conflicts in the mind can often be cleared up, too, by relaxing the tensions that have caused mental blocks. Some of this is accomplished by carrying the subject back to early memories.

These memories may have been pushed deep into the unconscious mind. But the relaxing power of hypnosis can bring them back within reach. Sigmund Freud, the founder of psychoanalysis, arrived at his revolutionary theories after early work with hypnosis. The technique of psychoanalysis, like that of hypnosis, consists of recovering buried memories from the unconscious.

Psychoanalysts try to uncover these memories by letting the patient relax and free his mind to wander as it wishes. This system, called free association, can gradually uncover many troubling memories one's conscious mind has been struggling to keep hidden. But free association cannot, by definition, be directed, so it is very slow. Hypnosis can speed up the process.

"Let us go back to the year when you were three years old," the hypnotist may say. "What happened then?" The memory of a childhood fright may uncover the cause of some deep fear—of the dark, or of being under water, perhaps. When the memory has been uncovered, the hypnotist will say, "Now when you wake up, you will have lost that fear." And with luck, it may be so.

Prenatal Recall

It is possible, in hypnosis, to dip back into deeply buried subconscious memories. Probably you can remember something of your first days at school. Possibly you can recall when you were learning to walk and talk. But under hypnosis some people have recalled hearing the doctor say, "It's a boy!" or "It's a girl!" at their own birth.

One young woman recalled that all the lights went off in the hospital at about the moment of her birth. When her mother was asked to confirm this, the mother was quite startled. She had entirely forgotten the incident, but on being reminded, she said, "Yes, that was so."

Of course it is possible that in earlier years this had been mentioned in the presence of the small child. But neither mother nor daughter remembered it before the hypnosis.

One prominent English psychiatrist says that some of his patients even remember, under hypnosis, being in their mothers' womb before birth and are able to describe their own births accurately.

Skeptics may argue that many people know enough about the birth process to be able to describe it. But the doctor in question has had patients who seemed to have no conscious knowledge of details of human reproduction. Still, they were able to give detailed descriptions of their birth. They knew whether the delivery had been difficult or easy. And their information was confirmed by medical records in hospitals or by their parents.

The psychiatrist who undertook these hypnoses has concluded that his patients could not all have "staged" the recollections under hypnosis. He feels that there is an element in human beings that is "capable of function even in the absence of a physical body." This is in agreement with the students of psychic phenomena who believe that each of us has double beings—one the physical, the other the astral or spirit being.

Only an independent spirit could account for memory of events occurring long before the brain and the nervous system of the body had completely evolved.

Past Lives Uncovered

A few people under hypnosis have gone back in memory before birth, to uncover hidden memories of past lives. Awake, they had no idea that these memories existed.

One woman, who had many memories of previous lives, recalled saying to herself as she was born, "Well, here I go again!"

Still another was reminded of her feeling of irritation at finding herself—her spirit—trapped in the helpless body of a baby.

In 1954 a young American woman underwent hypnosis and began to tell of her life in the early nineteenth century as an Irish girl named Bridey Murphy, of whom, when she was awake, she had never heard.

More recently an American novelist under hypnosis recalled a whole series of former lives stretching back to ancient Greece. It seemed that in her writing she had drawn on unconscious memories of those lives. But she had no memory of them, and when awake she did not believe in the rebirth, or reincarnation, of the soul.

Self-hypnosis and Yoga

It is possible to hypnotize oneself. Sometimes it happens accidentally, while one is listening to a monotonous rhythm that repeats itself over and over, or while driving on a long, straight, empty highway with nothing to watch and only the steady hum of your car's motor and tires to hear. This is a shallow kind of hypnosis in which one is still awake but not very alert—perhaps too relaxed for safety.

Yogis, people trained in the ancient Hindu art of yoga, put themselves into a trance by concentrating on their breathing or by clearing their minds and meditating on a saying repeated

many times. Some of them go into so deep a trance that they slow to an astonishingly low rate their breathing and heartbeat and all bodily functions.

Some yogis can so control their bodies that they can suck up into their rib cages all organs from their lower torsos. Or they can "turn off" their bodily functions so that for days or weeks they are rigid and motionless, as if dead. This state is called catalepsy and is ordinarily associated with severe mental illness. Then it is involuntary. But trained yogis have similar processes completely under the power of their wills. They believe that they can liberate themselves through spiritual discipline from what they consider the limitations of flesh, the delusions of sense and the pitfalls of thought.

There are tales such as the one of a south Indian yogi who was meditating one day on a riverbank when a flash flood swept down the stream, burying the yogi under a deep layer of mud. After some time a farmer began to plow this land. His plowshare struck something hard—the yogi. The farmer speedily uncovered the rigid form, at which time the yogi roused himself from his trance and walked away as if nothing had happened.

Certain yogis have practiced mass hypnosis on whole groups of followers. When one hears a story of a feast where thousands were fed by a yogi without a visible source of food supplies, or where river water was turned into butter, the simplest explanation is mass hypnosis or the power of suggestion pushed to its limit.

Dervishes and Fakirs

At almost the opposite end of the hypnotic scale from these often motionless yogis are dervishes—sometimes known as "whirling dervishes"—and fakirs. They, like the priests or shamans of Tibet and other parts of Asia, use the rhythms of drumbeats and dances to put themselves into trances.

So do men of some African tribes in religious ceremonies. These masked dancers also dance until they drop. Then they may speak in strange languages. It is believed that a divine spirit has entered into them.

It is this power of self-hypnosis that also makes it possible for certain men—usually belonging to an order of dervishes or fakirs—to walk barefoot over hot coals or to lie down on a bed of nail points without feeling any pain.

But just what is hypnotism? Ah, that is the mystery! Hundreds of years ago men who studied it thought it was animal magnetism. They believed that there was a magnetic fluid that came from all people. The theory was that some had the power to influence others by directing this fluid.

An Indian holy man has described the power behind psychic phenomena such as hypnosis as *prana*, a vital force in the air that "can be stored in the brain and nerve centers and transmitted to all parts of the body, much like an electric current." When a yogi breathes he absorbs the life energy of *prana* and thus may be able to live without food or drink for a long time.

About sixty-five years ago a learned writer trying to explain hypnosis said, "Very many so-called theories of hypnosis have been propounded, but few of them demand serious consideration." He himself leaned to a theory of "mental dissociation."

For decades in the mid-twentieth century hypnotism was scorned and scoffed at as a trick of stage magicians and parlor show-offs. But more recently, thanks to its healing powers, it has come into its own. Perhaps some day it will be truly understood.

Thought Transfer

A young woman sits in a plain, almost bare room, staring fixedly at a small bronze statue she holds in her hands. She fingers its curves lightly as she concentrates on it. In another room of the same building a second young woman lies on a cot. She is relaxed, dozing with eyes closed, hands folded lightly on her chest. But fastened to various points on her head—forehead, ears, temples, throat and the back of her skull—are small electrodes.

The two young women are students in a parapsychology laboratory. They are undertaking an experiment in a kind of extrasensory perception. The brain waves of the sleeping young woman on the laboratory cot are being charted by means of the electrodes. The experiment is being carefully timed.

Only when the brain-wave pattern indicated that the young woman was really asleep was the signal given for her partner in the experiment to go to work. The exact time was noted. Then a choice of several objects was offered to the "sender" of the psychic message. She chose the small bronze figure of a dancing Hindu god. Now she focuses on it with her eyes, and she adds the sense of touch by tracing the outlines of the figure with her fingers.

Slowly the pen lines charting her partner's alpha brain waves begin to jiggle. When they indicate lively activity the sleeper is awakened and asked what message she has received.

"Something small and hard," she says hesitantly. "Motion, lively motion, like a dance."

Those in charge are pleased. Surely this is much more than a chance description of the small bronze dancing figure this girl cannot even now see.

Controlled experiments of this sort are being conducted at several centers of study. They are part of an effort to assemble a body of statistical proof of extrasensory perception.

Extrasensory perception—or ESP—is the power to become aware of something without the help of any of the five senses—sight, hearing, taste, touch, smell. It may take any of a number of different forms.

Experiments like the one above involve thought transfer. This is communication from one mind to another without a sensory link between the minds. It is one form of extrasensory perception. The process of receiving a strong impression or communication from someone else's mind across a distance without the use of sense organs is also called telepathy. Usually it is referred to as "mental telepathy."

Thousands of examples have been reported. Here is one:

A college girl away from home for the first time awoke one night, hearing her grandmother call her name urgently. Restless and anxious, the girl waited until morning, then telephoned her home. She learned that her father had had a serious heart attack during the night. And her grandmother, forgetting in the stress of the moment that the girl was not at home, had indeed called out for her.

This example suggests what seem to be basic conditions required for thought transfer: The sender must develop tension and intensity; the receiver must be relaxed.

In another instance of telepathy, a man was at a late-afternoon meeting at which no telephone was available when he remembered that he had an appointment elsewhere at five o'clock. The hour was approaching, and he was distressed by the thought of the inconvenience his delay would cause his friend.

A young woman in the group noticed his concern and asked the cause. When he explained, she closed her eyes and sat quietly for a long moment. "Don't worry," she said as she opened her eyes. "The message has been delivered."

When the man checked later with his friend, he found that her telephone-answering service had received a message at a few minutes before five, saying that he would be delayed.

The college girl and her grandmother communicated without awareness of the technique of telepathy on the part of either of them. The young woman who apparently sent the message to the answering service was aware of her psychic power, but the recipient of the message was not. When both sender and receiver are consciously telepathically attuned, quite remarkable results can be achieved.

Forty years ago a rescue team went out in search of some aviators who had crashed in the Arctic. One man of the team kept a diary. He had also arranged with a friend at home that he would attempt to send telepathic messages at certain hours each week. The friend sat alone in his apartment at the appointed times and wrote whatever came into his mind. When the two men's writings were compared by a trained observer, it was found that 70 percent of the "scribblings" of the friend at home were identical to entries in the traveler's dairy.

Scientific investigation into telepathy suggests that its basis may lie in the alpha rhythm or alpha waves—the smooth rhythm of the electrical activity of the brain at rest. (The more rapid rhythm of the alert, wide-awake brain is called the beta rhythm.) Waves you send out, particularly in a moment of crisis, may affect the alpha rhythm of someone far away who is concerned about you, even if that person is not aware of having received a message.

Telepathy can be improved with training and practice. To learn to receive messages by thought transfer, one must be able to relax completely. Exercises such as those of yoga, which relax the muscles, slow heart action and regulate breathing, are very helpful to put one in a tranquil, receptive state. To learn to send messages by telepathy, one must practice concentrating one's mental powers, much as in performing hypnosis.

A good first experiment is to have one member of the team concentrate on sending a simple message. Let us say the message is "Walk across the room to the door, open it, then close it again." The sender should repeat this instruction silently to himself and at the same time picture the receiver following the instruction.

If the telepathy is working, the relaxed receiver may not be aware of receiving a message. He will simply have an urge to look out the door. But after he has opened the door it will seem natural to close it again.

One of the earliest controlled experiments in this kind of extrasensory perception involving thought transfer was carried on with decks of specially prepared cards. Each set contained twenty-five cards, five each of five designs:

crosses, circles, squares, stars and sets of waves. The theory behind the experiments with these cards was that if one simply guessed at the design on each card, without looking, chance would allow about five correct guesses of the twenty-five. If anyone could consistently, time after time, identify considerably more than five of twenty-five designs, it would strongly suggest that one had some special power.

Teams of two worked together in many of these experiments. They set their watches together. Then the two went into separate rooms. At an agreed-upon moment, one turned over a card from the pack and stared at the design, perhaps for several minutes. He concentrated all his thoughts on that design. In the other room his partner relaxed as completely as possible to clear his mind of confusing thoughts. Soon he wrote down what he thought the design was.

After several minutes the first experimenter turned over a second card and concentrated on it. His partner in the other room again wrote down the "message" he received as to its design. And so on through the pack.

Results were mixed. Some people apparently had no extrasensory power. Others got results well above what pure chance would have given them. Certain teams worked so well together that they consistently, through hundreds of rounds, "sent" and "received" eleven or twelve correct messages out of twenty-five —double the chance rate and more.

Some parapsychologists feel that this was an unnecessarily difficult test of mental powers beyond the five senses. They prefer to use solid objects that offer several different kinds of clues—color, material, weight, shape—as in the case of the metal dancing figure in the example at the beginning of this chapter—rather than just one abstract design in black on white.

Some of the most advanced work in this field has been done in the Soviet Union. Soviet teams a thousand miles or more apart have sent messages to one another using their minds alone.

And the messages—sometimes the description of an object or instructions such as "Turn on the light"—have been accurately received.

It is not always necessary for both people to be concentrating on an experiment. In an impressive number of cases people with psychic powers have willed an unsuspecting subject at a distance to fall asleep. And without even being aware of it, the person has dropped into a deep doze.

You may have at some time recognized a friend at a distance in a crowd and "willed" him to look at you, only to find him smiling and waving, with a look of pleased discovery on his face. These are possible examples of telepathy.

Whatever the power is, it does not seem to be restricted to human beings. One Russian psychic managed to give instructions to his trained dogs by telepathy. And some elephant trainers and scientists who have worked with these animals believe that elephants receive many of their instructions telepathically rather than through touch signals or the spoken word.

When scientists began to make controlled experiments with mental telepathy they hoped to learn what the force was that carried these messages through space—whether across a room or across many miles.

One theory proposed that it was an electromagnetic field. We live, after all, in the age of electronics. Without our control of electromagnetic forces we would not have telephones, telegraphs or television. It seemed logical that telepathy might also represent the work of some electromagnetic wave lengths that are not as yet understood.

Some men working with very high-frequency electromagnetic waves did report that these waves seemed to increase their sensitivity to mental communication. This suggestive finding was then put to a test.

A man who was known to be very good at telepathy was put into a lead-lined chamber. Lead is a non-conductor of electromagnetic waves. Still, sealed away from all known electronic forces, the man was able to receive telepathic messages. So evidently telepathy is not just an electromagnetic phenomenon.

The nature of the force that carries these messages is still a mystery to science. Some experimental workers refer to it as the "psi force." They hope some day to identify and understand it. At least today more and more people are willing to admit its existence!

Mysterious Sights and Sounds

The ability to "see" clearly in the mind's eye—often while asleep or in a trance state—things beyond the range of one's physical experience is called clairvoyance, "clear seeing." Here is a reported example:

A mother whose son was at sea suddenly had a vision of his ship being rammed by another vessel and of her son clinging to a raft. Within days she received word that her son's ship had indeed been rammed—at the time of her vision—and that her son was among those saved on life rafts.

If one "hears" things by unexplained means, this power is called clairaudience. For example, a minister, while napping before an evening service some years ago, dreamed of a certain hymn. In the dream he heard voices calling out urgently above the sound of rushing waters. The dream was so vivid and disturbing that at the end of the service that evening the minister asked the congregation to join him in singing the hymn.

The words of the hymn ran in part as follows: "Hear, Father, while we pray to Thee/For those in peril on the sea."

At the time of that evening service, far away on the North Atlantic, the steamship *Titanic* was sinking, carrying hundreds of people to their deaths.

Thirty years before that, a Boston newspaper reporter saw and heard, in a dream of vivid and horrifying detail, the explosion of the Indonesian island of Krakatoa—one of the most immense and destructive volcanic eruptions ever known.

He was so deeply moved by the dream that he wrote down his experience in full when he awoke. As days passed and news slowly filtered out of the stricken area, the details of the nightmare the reporter had experienced halfway

around the world were found to be perfectly accurate. In his dream he had been both clairvoyant and clairaudient.

Again, a man driving quietly along a familiar road suddenly felt a terrible, crushing pain in his chest. Fearing a heart attack, he stopped the car; but the pain ebbed, and he drove on home. There he soon received word that his son had been killed in an automobile crash. At the very moment when the father had experienced the strange and terrifying pain, the young man's chest had been crushed.

The father's experience could be classified as clairsentience—a mysterious clear sensing of a situation taking place at a distance.

Sometimes the message is less vivid but still urgent. A woman driving at some distance from her home had a sudden compulsion to turn and go back. Arriving, she found her home in flames.

Other experiences combine thought transfer with clairvoyance and clairaudience. All these powers to send or receive information without the use of the senses are closely related.

During World War II, for example, a mother whose son was in the South Pacific dreamed that a palm tree was blown onto the tent in which he was sleeping. In her dream she called his name aloud, which woke her with a vivid memory of the dream.

Not long afterward she received a letter from her son telling of a strange experience he had had. In his sleep he had heard his mother call to him so clearly that, still half asleep, he ran from the tent in response to the call. At that moment a palm tree fell onto the tent, crushing the cot on which he had been sleeping.

Countless examples such as these could be cited. To many people—as in the examples above—the power comes only once. Clairvoyance and clairaudience do not seem to be powers that can be consciously developed.

One famous clairvoyant had been an undistinguished house painter until one day at work

against the piling of a pier jutting out from the wooded shore of a small lake. She described the scene so vividly and precisely that the parents recognized it at once. Searchers sent to the spot found the child's body just as the clairvoyant had described it.

The existence of clairvoyance has been adequately proved by the accuracy of many visions. One young man in whose town a brutal murder had been committed had a clairvoyant nightmare in which he saw a respected local citizen committing the murder. He hesitated to mention his dream except to his wife but did at last; and the man seen in the dream soon confessed to the murder.

Another clairvoyant offered his help to police in solving a crime. They laughed at him until he told one of the policemen in detail what he—the policeman—had in his uniform pocket. The list was so accurate that the police shamefacedly accepted the clairvoyant's help. They were soon glad they had.

he fell, striking his head. From that day on he had an amazing power.

Taken once to the scene of a fire that had clearly been started by an arsonist, he found a charred screwdriver handle in the ashes. He handled it for a moment, then described the boy who had started the fire. When some group pictures of boys in the community were shown to him, he pointed out one boy as the firebug. Then he said that a box of matches and some lighter fluid would be found in the boy's pockets, though the boy did not smoke. When the youth he had identified was questioned, sure enough, the matches and lighter fluid were right in his pockets.

This kind of clairvoyant vision, when it is spurred by the handling of some related object, is called psychometry.

Another recognized clairvoyant was consulted by the despairing parents of a missing child. She "saw" the child's small body wedged

Contacts with Spirits

When a shy teen-age girl who had neither enemies nor suitors vanished nearly twenty years ago, her family naturally was distressed and anxious. Weeks passed without any word of her. Then her brother heard of a man who had located missing jewelry by some psychic power and might be able to be of help.

The man agreed to try, and fifty persons, including a police officer, gathered to witness the attempt. For some minutes the psychic sat in silence, breathing heavily, with closed eyes. Then he began to speak—in the voice of a terrified young girl.

She reported that she had been attacked and killed by a man whom she named. And she told where her body could be found.

According to the report, the psychic subsequently led the police not only to the body but to the murder weapon, hidden by the murderer in a shed behind his home. The murderer himself was arrested in the house and soon confessed to the crime.

A Message in Shorthand

A story is told of a four-year-old boy who played quietly on the floor of his home with pencil and paper. Quiet play was in order because the child's father had very recently died, and his mother was deeply grieved.

The lad's scribbling was lying on the floor when a friend of the family arrived. By chance he glanced at the scribbling and cried out in surprise. For it resembled strongly an old-fashioned kind of shorthand, long since abandoned, that the friend and the dead father had studied years before.

The friend could not read the message—if there was one—though he recognized some of the word forms. But he was sufficiently interested to ask permission to take the paper to someone who would be familiar with the old shorthand system.

Soon he was back with the incredible news that the small boy's scribbling contained a message from the dead father to his wife, telling her the location of a safe-deposit box she did not know about. The box was found just as the spirit hand had promised.

Eastern Psychic Wisdom

Parapsychology is the name given to the study of these and other mental phenomena that cannot be explained by natural laws. It is growing as a legitimate research field in reputable universities. This growth reflects a recent upsurge of interest in psychic phenomena which, in the Western world, used to be lightly dismissed by most of the public as fakery.

In its reluctant acceptance of the reality of extrasensory perception, the Western world is far behind Eastern lands such as India and Tibet. There psychic powers have long been accepted and have been widely used by whole groups of trained yogis, lamas and others.

Among African tribal peoples, too, priests, medicine men and other leaders have been selected at least in part for their psychic ability. And they have been trained in such skills as mind reading (a great help in exposing thieves and other criminals) and thought transfer.

Travelers in these lands have often been amazed to find when they arrived in a village that they were expected, though that village had no contact by telephone, telegraph or other known means of communication with the outside world.

A trained psychologist from an American university was traveling in India recently with a

group of people interested in meditation and psychic powers. They were on a long day's bus trip; it was late in the afternoon and everyone was getting tired. They were looking forward to a hot meal and a night's rest, though they had no hotel reservations and did not know where they would be staying.

One of the men suggested that they make a short side trip to see the grounds where a great religious festival had recently been held. The psychologist, who was in charge of the trip, did not want to go, claiming it would take too much time. Then he reconsidered, deciding it would not take very long and might be interesting.

He was not aware of having received a message or instructions, nor was the man who had made the suggestion. But when the bus reached the deserted festival grounds it was met by the guru under whom the American had started his study of meditation but whom he had not seen for many months.

The guru had food ready for the whole busload and places prepared for them all to sleep. He had been expecting their exact number long before they were aware of being headed for this spot.

What paths his thought waves traveled is still a mystery—at least to us in the West.

Spiritualism— Seances and Mediums

In the mid-1800s there lived in a small town in New York State two young girls—Kate and Margaret Fox by name—who were to gain wide fame through their apparent ability to communicate with spirits. It all started with a series of mysterious rappings in the home where the Fox family lived. Soon the girls found that they could ask questions and receive answers in the form of raps—one for no, three for yes.

From this modest beginning came a long series of presumed contacts with the spirits of dead relatives, friends and eminent persons. In general a spirit wishing to contact someone in the world of the living must, it seems, use someone with psychic powers as a go-between. "Medium" came to be the term used to describe these people, and Kate Fox was the first to win fame as a medium.

Within a few years a good many other individuals discovered or developed within themselves ability to act as mediums. "Spirit circles" gathered for the purpose of contacting individuals in the spirit world became a fashion in England, the United States and parts of western Europe in the latter half of the 1800s. Table-tilting, automatic writing and speaking from trances were among the techniques employed. Belief in spiritualism, centered on faith in life after death and in the ability of spirits in the afterworld to communicate with the living, became a religion for many people.

People who have proclaimed themselves to be mediums have been much in demand. They have often gathered about them followers who were willing to pay sizable sums for the privilege of attending a seance at which spirits of the dead were supposed to be contacted. Unfortunately the lure of fame and fortune attracted many people without any real psychic powers who used all sorts of tricks and gadgets with which to arrange fake "appearances" of spirits. Hidden lights, mirrors, balloons and fans to stir up currents of air gave the illusion of ghostly appearances. Trick tables and systems of wires permitted false mediums to simulate table tapping and other sounds through which spirits were said to communicate.

In addition, psychic powers are admittedly fluctuating in nature. Even in the case of people whose unexplainable talents are admitted by the most skeptical there are times when the mysterious forces fail them. When one has developed a reputation and following there is an obvious temptation to produce results—particularly when the audience is paying to see marvels. This has caused many spiritualists to indulge in fraud or trickery to enhance their images. Even with these imposters, however, the mysterious powers of some individuals cannot be explained away.

Table Tapping and Trances

In many popular seances a small group gathers around a table in a dimly lighted room. They hold hands in a circle around the table so that no one can use a hand without a neighbor being aware of it. Upon occasion it is reported that a whole group turned their chairs with backs to the table, then knelt on the seats, with their hands joined on the chair backs. Still, the table tilted, tapping out yes or no answers to questions in a code that had been agreed on.

In addition to table tappings, flashing of lights, ringing of bells, playing of musical instruments (all without the apparent touch of human hands), the movement of objects, tying or untying of knots and other wondrous activities have been credited to spirits.

Many mediums use no lights, bells, tables or other mechanical gadgets. They simply fall into trances and speak in strange voices. Presumably these voices belong to someone in the spirit world. The spirit may be that of a person familiar to one of the group, with a message for that person. More often it is said to be the voice of a "control," a sort of spirit-world medium or go-between, who passes on messages on behalf of other spirits who cannot "bridge the gap."

A true medium has no recollection, when he or she comes out of a trance, of what has been said or done during the trance. The medium may even be impervious to pain from pin pricks or lighted matches. These trances may be described as a form of self-hypnosis.

Whatever the force at work may be, it cannot be denied that in some instances, in the presence of skeptical, scientifically trained men, mediums have passed on messages, by voice or in writing, that were entirely outside their scope of knowledge. In many cases the person receiving the message learned something from the message which he or she had not known before, which also rules out thought transfer.

Thus, one medium described a young woman whom she claimed to see in spirit form saying, "I'm going now and taking the baby with me." Someone in the group recognized the description as that of a young married cousin. Soon after, word came to him of the cousin's death in childbirth; the baby died with her.

Very frequently, it seems, the spirits which are seen or spoken to are newly dead. They want to give word of their passing or to be in touch once more with someone dear to them. For example, a man reported some twenty-five years ago that as he lay in bed one night his father, whose home was 1,000 miles away, walked in the door. The son was rather surprised to see that his father was wearing work clothes, which he usually wore only when doing odd jobs around the house. The older man sadly pressed his son's hand. Then with a shake of his head he vanished. Next day news came that the father had died suddenly while working on his car. He was wearing, at the time, exactly the work costume in which his spirit had paid its call.

Some years earlier an Englishman reported that a spirit voice spoke to him at a seance, claiming to be his father, who had been dead seven years. When the son seemed skeptical, the spirit voice referred to a matter known only to the father, son and one other friend, also dead. Soon the friend's spirit also appeared, gave his name and continued the conversation about the topic known only to the three of them.

A particularly interesting spirit message was received by a well-known English woman medium in 1930. She was in a trance when the spirit of a flight lieutenant supposedly spoke through her. He said he wanted to report the cause of the crash of the experimental dirigible of which he had been the commander and in which he had met his death.

The report proved to be very technical. It was taken down in shorthand and was subsequently sent to the Air Ministry. Officials there confirmed that many details tallied exactly with the facts as gathered by an investigation of the crash, though the medium had no knowlege of this highly technical field.

On other occasions another medium passed on, at a single sitting, messages from thirty or more spirits in a succession of different voices. Many of the messages concerned details known only to one person in the group at the seance.

Even the most skeptical observer had to agree that it would have been almost impossible for a faker to keep all this information straight, even if it had been possible to assemble it. And the assembling would have been practically impossible, since no one knew just who might come to the seance on any particular evening.

Some of the most amazing spirit manifestations have been those when spirits could be seen, at least hazily, moving about in the room. On a few of these occasions photographs were taken; they showed the spirit forms and also the medium, who remained in his proper place in the group.

Dogs, cats and other animals have been made to appear. Plants have dropped down onto the table around which groups were seated. Even though rooms were sealed with tape, or the members of the circle were chained together to rule out trickery, still, spirits seemed to appear—perhaps only heads or hands.

One such occasion had been carefully checked and controlled by skeptics. At the end of the seance, when the lights came on, it was discovered that the medium was no longer present. He was soon found in another room, some distance away, still in a trance.

Examples of contacts with spirits could be multiplied. There are many people who believe firmly in the possibility of contacting the spirits of those who have died. It is interesting to note, however, that several enthusiastic believers who are now dead, such as Sir Arthur Conan Doyle, creator of Sherlock Holmes, promised to contact friends from "the beyond" if it were possible. Years have passed, but no one has reported having heard from them.

Ouija and Automatic Writing

Hold a pencil loosely in writing position above a blank sheet of paper. Your grip should be too loose for you to control the pencil, but it should be in a writing position. Now relax and empty your mind as much as possible of all thoughts. For some time nothing will happen. Persevere and, if you are lucky and have a touch of the psychic in your makeup, the pencil may quiver and begin to move slowly of its own volition—still supported by your hand.

As a pleasant and intriguing parlor trick, automatic writing may draw upon a level just below your conscious mind. A woman engaged to be married received a message from her pencil: "Forget Franz [her fiancé]; marry Ted." Clearly this was no more than a hint from her unconscious—a hint which, in this instance, she did not heed.

At a deeper psychic level, automatic writing may draw upon material of which the writer is unaware. One such happening followed the death of Charles Dickens in 1870. Dickens had been writing a novel, The Mystery of Edwin Drood. At the time of his death, six installments had been published, but no one could find as much as a note to hint at the solution the author had planned.

Two years later, a lighthearted and light-minded young American printer's helper with only about a fifth-grade education and no apparent literary talent drifted into a New England town. For about a year he sat in on seances in the parlor of his landlady. Then he announced to her that Charles Dickens had commissioned him, from the spirit world, to finish The Mystery of Edwin Drood.

The landlady agreed to provide him with room and board while he completed the task. For several months the young man spent many hours writing, often furiously, in his room, absorbed in a trance. He explained that he was simply writing from Dickens' dictation.

News of the project leaked out, and it was soundly ridiculed. But within a year the completed novel appeared in bookshops. And the most skeptical critics had to agree that it was precisely in the style and vocabulary of Charles Dickens—and not at all the sort of thing the young printer's apprentice could possibly have turned out on his own.

After this feat he faded once again into the ranks of undistinguished working men. But the mystery of his relationship with the spirit of Charles Dickens has never been explained.

Oscar Wilde, another English writer, also presumably made contact from the spirit world. He did not undertake any creative work through the medium he "used" but carried on a lengthy series of conversations in the caustic and colorful style he had employed in life.

Taylor Caldwell, a well-known American novelist, has said that at least one of her novels was virtually dictated by a presence that guided her hands as she typed.

Other examples of creative "automatic writing" could be mentioned. The most intriguing literary accomplishments from the spirit world, though, started with a contact through a ouija board.

A ouija board has printed on it the letters of the alphabet, numbers from one to ten, yes, no and "goodbye." A small heart-shaped board called a planchette, raised on casters, is placed on the larger board. Two persons put their fingertips lightly on the planchette and then ask a question.

With luck, the planchette will soon quiver and start to move of its own accord. It may answer the question with a yes, a no or a number, or spell out a longer answer letter by letter.

Often, as with automatic writing, the answers seem to be guided by the subconscious mind—or the imagination—of the people working the board. But occasionally, when someone properly attuned comes along, a ouija board (the name combines the French and German words for "yes") produces extraordinary results.

One of the most amazing experiences on record started in 1913 when a young woman in St. Louis was persuaded to try a ouija board. It might be mentioned that there had been some psychic experiences in her family, but this particular young woman did not consider herself at all psychic. Nor was she interested in the field.

She tried out the board several times without any great success. Then suddenly one evening the board whizzed briskly about, spelling out "Many moons ago I lived. Again I come. Patience Worth is my name."

This was the opening of a spirit relationship that lasted for years. A friend began to write down every word Mistress Patience spelled out. And what words! Patience Worth had lived, she indicated, in the seventeenth century and was quick-witted and full of stories.

Gradually the letter-by-letter ouija-board method of communication became slow and laborious. Then Patience spoke directly through the young woman, while a friend took down every word and later typed up the material.

By this means they produced six complete novels and many poems, as well as reams of other witty material that seemed quite outside the experience and beyond the skill and mental power of the medium.

Numerous visitors came to observe the sittings over the years. One professor insisted that Patience must be a creation of the medium's subconscious mind. To almost everyone else this seemed impossible, since the young woman had dropped out of high school in her first year, had no intellectual interests and no apparent writing talent on her own.

What was the explanation? When Patience was asked, she said, "I hae said it be a trick of throbbin'. The wench be attuned unto the throb o' me . . . save I find an harp 'pon which to lean, I am mute."

Since the death of her faithful medium, Patience Worth has been true to her words.

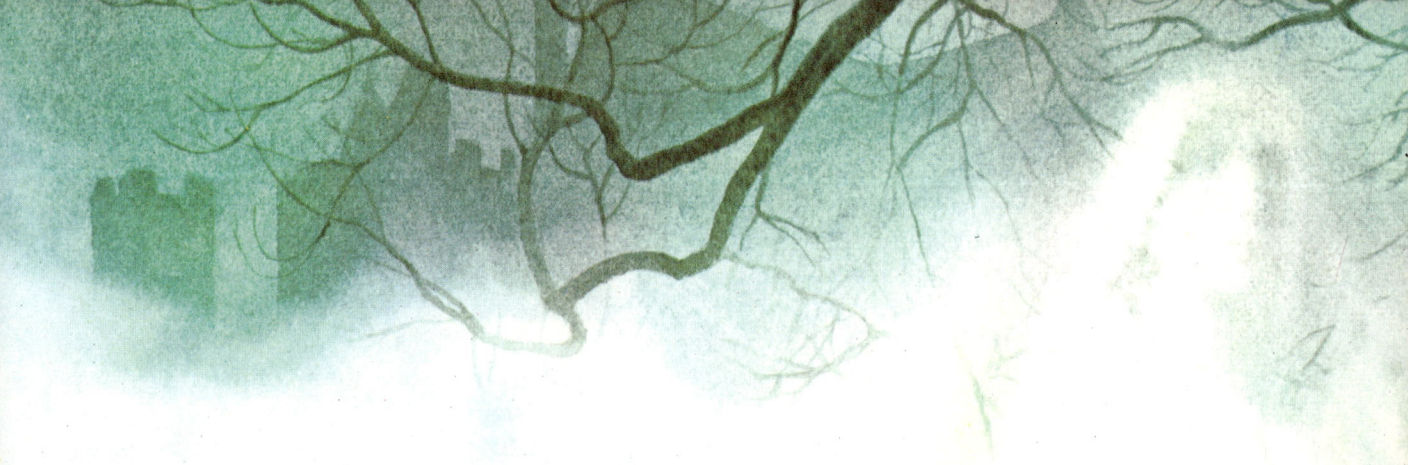

Ghostly Apparitions and Poltergeists

Retire for the night to an unfamiliar bedroom in an old, old house in England or Ireland, with heavy draperies at the windows, creaking floorboards and a candle guttering at your bedside. The possibility may well cross your mind that you may be awakened by a ghostly presence.

There are many old homes said to be haunted by the restless, mournful spirits of lovely, sad young women or gloomy gentlemen in outmoded clothing. Some died young, betrayed in love. Many met violent deaths—like the onetime queen of England, Anne Boleyn, whose spirit is said to wander the Tower of London, the macabre outline of a decapitated head beneath its ghostly arm. Others wander too, mourning for a lost child or mate. So many of these apparitions have been seen, by skeptics as well as by superstitious souls, that many people think there is very likely some truth to them.

These unhappy souls seem to be imprisoned in settings they knew in life. Some are said to be freed from their imprisonment by the efforts —sometimes called "rescue work"—of a psychic medium who is able to give them peace. Others are exorcised—driven away—by special religious ceremonies.

Ghosts reportedly do not appear only to lone watchers, nor only in the darkness. Some appear in midday and before whole groups of people. Most often this happens when a spirit newly departed from its body wishes to inform someone that death has come to a friend or relative. The newly dead spirit may have an urgent message to convey—in one case, at least, the location of a missing will. Or the spirit may, it appears, wish to be in touch with a dear one once more before departing.

In one account, a woman newly widowed stopped with her sister at a restaurant after the funeral of her husband. As they waited to be served she was surprised to hear a man at a nearby table say to his companion, "Why, isn't that Bill?" (her husband's name). She looked around and saw the shadowy form of her late husband standing beside her table, smiling sadly. As she tried to speak, he vanished.

A young man on his way to pay a visit to an older couple he knew very slightly had a pleasant conversation with a pretty young woman during a short train ride. When he mentioned where he was going she said, "Oh, how interesting. I used to live there."

Over tea, after his arrival, he mentioned the encounter to his host and hostess. They grew pale and exchanged mournful glances. Then they told him that the young woman he had described—and of whom he drew a pencil sketch—had been their daughter who had recently died.

A good many reported ghosts have been identified by means of portraits made during their lifetimes that remained in their old homes. In some cases it seems possible that the portraits themselves overstimulated the imaginations of guests. But that could scarcely account for one authenticated sighting of a ghost in a small town in northern England.

There, in 1931, an old home was to be opened to the public as a landmark. On the day of the opening ceremony, as a trumpet sounded, a gentleman dressed in medieval garb appeared in an open upper window of the house. He remained in full view long enough to be seen by many of the inhabitants of the village.

Only later did someone locate a centuries-old painting of the original owner of the home. And all the villagers agreed that it was he whom they had seen in the open window.

The superstition that ghosts haunt graveyards seems to have little foundation. The spirits of the dead seem rather to revisit the scenes of their life. A well-loved grandfather thus was seen a number of times over a period of months by various members of the family. One child so small that she would not yet have heard of ghosts was heard addressing the spirit by name.

Poltergeists

Poltergeists, "noisy ghosts," generally do not appear in visible form. Instead they are said to bang door knockers, open and close windows, set chairs to rocking, smash glasses and toss pebbles at windows. They are also said to hurl furniture around, upset bottles of water or other liquids, toss food onto the floor and be a nuisance or real torment to whole families.

In one situation several observers spoke to the poltergeists that were rapping in walls. The people succeeded in getting answers to questions—two raps for no, three for yes.

Encouraged by this success, one man put a hand in his jacket pocket and asked the spirit to rap out the number of fingers he was holding out on the concealed hand. Back came the correct answer in a brisk set of raps.

Experiences with poltergeists have been recorded for many centuries. Mysterious showers of stones from clear air were reported as long ago as A.D. 355—and as recently as a year or so ago. The most recent report came from young ski instructors at a mountain resort. They said that the stones floated down instead of falling freely and caused no damage. Some of the stones were warm to the touch, others icy cold.

Floating stones from the sky seem fairly harmless. But some poltergeists reportedly have ripped clothes from young people, pulled their hair or flung them roughly to the floor.

One really bothersome poltergeist, who claimed to be the spirit of a murderer hanged fifty years or more ago, tormented the family of a reporter who had covered his trial—and whose wife was, as it happened, rather psychic. Footsteps prowled their home, disturbing the family dogs. Windows were broken, and furniture was tossed about in the rooms. A casserole being baked for dinner was taken from the oven and its contents were dumped on the floor though no one was in the room.

Finally, in the middle of the night, unseen hands tried to strangle the wife. Wakened by her agonized sounds, her husband thought at first that she was having some sort of seizure. Then he saw on her neck and throat the imprint of powerful hands. After that, the couple abandoned not only the house but the country.

There were no children or young people in this family, but poltergeists generally seem to direct their attention to one person, often—though by no means always—a child. One theory is that tensions in the psychic energy of the child, or adult, cause the weird activities.

Recently a family in the United States was harassed by malicious poltergeists. Since they could not readily give up their home or leave the community, they called on a Catholic priest to perform the rite of exorcism. Some Christian sects other than Catholicism also have formal ceremonies or rites of exorcism to drive out evil spirits or devils.

What Is a Ghost?

Many people interested in psychic phenomena believe that every human being has a double form. One is the outer, physical form we are accustomed to seeing. The other is the inner, spirit form, sometimes called the astral body. Other names are also given to it, but its composition is not really understood, even by those who believe it it most firmly.

Some psychics say that this astral body has a substance that they can see—and feel. These psychics claim that this substance is what leaves the body at death. Moved by very intense emotion, the astral body may materialize as a ghost. It is this same "life force" or psychic energy that can cause poltergeist activities.

The moving of objects by psychic powers, which is a central part of poltergeist activities, is called psychokinesis. A good many psychics who are trying to learn to control their special mental powers have made great efforts to master psychokinesis. But it remains a very rare ability.

A very few strongly psychic personalities are reported to have made a musical instrument play in an empty room and to have caused furniture to move about without anyone near it. But very few people can move so much as a book of matches without using any physical force. In one set of scientific experiments it did seem that a few people could influence the fall of dice by their thoughts.

The art—or magic—of producing a ghostly apparition is equally elusive. We know of no scientific experiments that have produced a ghost. That process is still a mystery.

Travel Outside the Body

Do you like to travel but feel that it takes too much time and money? Perhaps astral travel is the way you should go. All you need to do is will your spirit form out of your physical body. Then without being troubled by walls or other barriers, without any need for an airplane, you can go where you wish.

If you should be "seen" on your astral travels, while your physical being is known to be somewhere else, the vision seen is called a *doppelgänger*, a German word meaning "doublegoer." But spirits on astral travels are not always visible.

Tibetan lamas, we are told, have been trained to use this method of travel and have done so for centuries. An occasional Westerner discovers, usually accidentally, that he or she has this power of astral flight, though few people can call upon it at will.

One young woman reported, for example, that while she was living in the eastern United States she decided that she would very much like to see a sister in California. It had been some years since they had been together.

As she dozed one evening she felt herself slipping through the walls of the room where she lay. Then she was aware of the wind whipping around her and of the stars in the night sky. Soon she heard the soft slosh of surf on a shore. She saw a quiet street lined with neat small houses and soon found herself on the porch of a house she had never seen before.

This was not where her sister had been living when they had last been together several years before! But through the window she saw her sister moving about a room and clearly noted what she was wearing.

Next day, safely back in her own quarters, the young woman wrote to her sister, reporting this experience. She carefully marked the letter "Please Forward" as she addressed it to the sister's latest address of which she knew.

Sure enough, the reply came from a new address. And, yes, the house and street were just as the astral visitor had seen them, and the sister did have a dress that fit the description.

Sherman's March to the Sea

To reach farther back in time, there was a young woman who, during the Civil War, had an interesting astral journey that has been recorded. This young woman, whose home was in the North, became dissatisfied with news coverage of the progress of General Sherman's march to the sea. So, as she later reported, she decided in her sleep that she would visit him.

She was aware of traveling, of lifting the flap of the general's tent and of his telling her that the campaign was going very badly.

At breakfast, back home the next morning, she reported the experience to her family in detail, including a description of the informal costume General Sherman was wearing when she talked with him.

The family noted the date of the astral visit. And news reports within a few days confirmed the gloomy word she had received.

Years later a magazine article by an army officer who had served with General Sherman during that campaign mentioned the general's gloomy mood on the night in question—and even described the exact costume the young woman had said that the general was wearing.

Learning Astral Travel

The power to travel outside the body can be developed, it seems, by some people who have

psychic force in abundance. More than one report exists of people who have trained themselves through concentration to be able to slip away from their bodies—and return again.

One man who had been working on this decided that he would try to visit, astrally, a young woman he knew. Moreover, he would see if he could make her aware of his visit. For several weeks he tried, unsuccessfully. Then one day when he had been working late and was very tired he slumped down at his desk to relax for a moment and made one more attempt.

A few days later he happened to meet the young woman casually. She told him with some amusement that she had seen him recently. She had dozed off in the easy chair in her room after a hard day. She awoke to find her friend standing beside her chair. He had not seemed to be aware of her, she said, and walked toward the door. But before he reached the door he vanished. She was able to report correctly just what suit he had been wearing on his astral visit.

Perhaps you have at some time been with someone who seemed to fall into a trance. Someone else may have said, "Old So-and-So looks as if he's a thousand miles from here." Possibly he was.

Astral projection demands such complete relaxation that it is most often accomplished in sleep. Some people believe that if you wake with a terrific jerk and a feeling of falling, it may be that you were forced to return your spirit body to your physical body too quickly because of some outside intrusion. The shock, according to this explanation, can be a bit painful.

Some experts think there is danger in rousing anyone too quickly from sleep, or in particular from a trance—including sleepwalking. In the forced transition the "silver cord" that allegedly joins the spirit or astral self to the physical body might be broken. Death could be the result.

Some years ago there were reports of a number of deaths from unexplained causes —mainly in the Philippines. Apparently the deaths were triggered by nightmares. It is possible that the breaking of this silver cord was the mysterious cause.

A Laboratory Test

If astral projection seems a bit too far out for you to take seriously, consider this. In the parapsychology laboratory of a West Coast university of great renown, a man dozed on a cot with electrodes fastened to his head. He was the subject of a controlled experiment in astral projection. He had been chosen because he was said to have the ability to travel outside his body.

Against one wall of the small room, close to the ceiling, an open-topped box had been tacked. The box was a couple of feet down from the ceiling but high enough so that no one standing on the floor of the room could look inside.

In the box was a selection of small objects. This time (the objects were changed each time the experiment was tried) they might have included a red pencil, a stapler, a roll of postage stamps and a small scissors. Another time the box might have contained an assortment of playing cards placed face up.

The man on the cot had no way of knowing the objects in the box. No one who did know was present, so there could be no possibility of thought transfer. But as he slept, abruptly the pattern of brain waves recorded by the electrodes changed. Some activity was going on in his mind. It might have been a dream. Or it might have been an astral projection.

The psychologists conducting the experiment waited until the brain-wave pattern returned to a quiet, steady line. Then they roused the sleeper and asked him what was in the box near the ceiling. The contents, remember, could be seen only from a position high up in the room.

Without hesitation the man listed the objects in the box—time after time, set after different set, just as he somehow saw them there.

This was an experiment in astral projection—or some other mysterious force—that had been carefully supervised by trained psychologists!

Levitation

A young man deep in a hypnotic trance lies stretched out on several straight chairs. Around him stand several men, each with the forefinger of one hand outstretched. These men synchronize their breathing. When they are breathing in unison, they place their outstretched forefingers under the body of the hypnotized friend. Then at a signal—let us say on the intake of a breath—all together they raise their arms. The sleeping young man's body rises lightly into the air, supported only by those fingertips.

This is a form of levitation. The word "levitation" simply means that something is made light or buoyant. In this case, psychic power is used to make a heavy body buoyant enough to be easily supported in the air.

In the latter years of the nineteenth century and the early years of the twentieth century, when spiritualism was much in the news, levitation was a popular parlor trick along with table tapping and the calling up of spirits by a sensitive medium.

Numerous stories, presumably authentic, tell of men who, whether influenced by other strongly psychic personalities or just by their own or someone else's concentrations of mental powers, could sit cross-legged, usually while in a trance, and rise several inches or even feet above the ground. Often these occurrences were credited to India, for yoga exercises are known to develop great control over bodily activities.

One yogi permitted his levitation to be studied and photographed. Lying full length on the ground, he rose a few inches into the air—but only for a second. The scientist observing him felt that he had simply (or not so simply!) trained all his muscles to cooperate in bouncing him into the air.

In the West, levitation has in recent years been looked upon as a work of sleight of hand or other trickery. It has therefore been scorned by most people taking a scientific approach.

In lands like India and Tibet, however, levitation has been taken for granted. Not everyone, of course, has the power. But skilled yogis and highly trained Tibetan lamas or priests are taught levitation. Even by them it is not very highly thought of, it seems. In one book describing the education of lamas, levitation is dismissed with a rather backhanded comment. Of course it is possible to move through the air, the writer says. But why would anyone bother when it is so much simpler to travel by astral projection, without the burden of a physical body?

Before discounting levitation entirely, though, one should consider the case of Daniel Douglas Home, a famous medium of the 1860s. The report claims that one day in a trance he left the room where several of his friends were gathered for a seance. They heard the window being opened in the next room; then, to their astonishment, Home appeared *outside* the window of the room in which they sat, some seventy feet above the ground. Standing in thin air, he opened the window and reentered the room.

One of the men present closed the window, observing to the group that it had not been opened more than a foot. He could not understand how Home had been able to enter through so small an opening, even in a trance.

At this, Home went out the window again, head first through the narrow opening and rigid as a board. Soon he reappeared, feet first, and returned to the group.

When he awoke from his trance, he did not seem to remember any part of the experience. Some who heard of it wondered if all the others present might have been hypnotized and led to believe they had seen something that never really happened. But in all the years of Home's activities as a psychic—during which he was observed to rise, unsupported, from the ground or floor more than a hundred times—no one ever discovered him playing a trick. So the whole matter of levitation is still a mystery with, perhaps, some basis in fact.

Foreknowledge

At the small boy's cry, his mother awoke and hurried to his bedside. The four-year-old was sitting up in bed, shaking from a nightmare. As his mother soothed him, he explained that he had seen his father in some water with tall grass all around, and it had frightened him.

Two day later the boy's father was duck hunting with a brother-in-law when their boat capsized. The brother-in-law drowned, but the father saved himself by clinging to tall reeds.

This is just one of the countless recorded examples of a strange phenomenon sometimes called precognition, also known as *déjà vu*, French for "already seen." A dictionary defines this as "the illusion of having already experienced something actually being experienced for the first time." But to many it seems more in the nature of a warning than an illusion.

Thus, one stormy evening a woman facing a long drive home along a dreary road through desolate country said to her husband, "Please let's stay here overnight. I have a feeling of trouble connected with that drive." Since the weather was very bad, the husband humored her by spending the night where they were. Next morning they discovered a flaw in their automobile that caused a serious breakdown within a few miles. Had they started out on that stormy night drive, they would have faced a grim night stuck on a desolate stretch of road.

Another classic tale is that of the man who dreamed of a black coach drawing up beside him. The coachman called out, "Step lively. Get on board!" and cracked his whip over the horses' backs. Then, as the horrified dreamer watched, he drove the coach straight off a cliff.

Next day the dreamer, having forgotten his "experience" of the night before, started off for his usual bus ride to work. As he waited at his customary corner, a bus drew up beside him, and an unfamiliar driver called out, "Step lively." Glancing up, the man on the curb recognized the coachman of his dream. With a start of horror, he stepped back and waved the bus on. Before it had gone many blocks it was involved in a terrible smashup.

Then there was the case of the prominent movie actor, chatting with his wife out on the lawn of their home, who suddenly shouted, "Run for shelter." His wife obeyed, and he joined her. A moment later a small plane crashed in flames at the spot where they had been. The actor had somehow "seen" the crash in his mind's eye moments before it actually happened.

Premonitions

Most of us have had the feeling at one time or another of having been warned by an inner voice against doing something or other. We call these premonitions, a term based on the Latin phrase meaning "forewarning." Usually they are based on barely subconscious fear or dread. Usually circumstances force us to do what we dreaded or feared, and it works out perfectly well. Our premonition comes to nothing and we forget it. If by chance it comes true, we remember it, though, and tell it as a strange and wonderful "psychic" happening.

Even stronger than the kind of vague warning experienced in a premonition is precognition or foreknowledge. Some so-called precognitions can be shrugged away as the kind of chance happening or coincidence that accounts for many premonitions. But others are so vivid, and bring such a shock of recognition of something that has gone before, that they suggest to some students of the psychic that time may not be the "never-ending stream" of the poet's line, flowing smoothly along. Instead, it may be a complex fabric that occasionally gathers into "wrinkles." This process, over which human beings apparently have no control, may result in one's mental self perceiving an experience in advance of the physical self.

The "wrinkle in time" theory is satisfying to some students of psychic phenomena. To others, though, these moments when we turn a corner in a strange town and suddenly know just what we will find on the street ahead, or enter a strange house and feel it strangely familiar, have a different meaning. They suggest that we are returning to a scene we have known in some past life.

Reincarnation: Have You Lived Before?

In a trance, a young Englishwoman began some years ago to tell her experiences as a girl at the royal court of ancient Egypt. Her husband, fascinated, took down all she told him. And as the trances continued, the "memories" became a novel.

Had the soul of the young woman in England really lived before in the body of a young Egyptian? However unlikely according to current knowledge, the Englishwoman was convinced that this was so. In fact, she believed that she had had more than a hundred incarnations—lives in different bodies.

The belief in reincarnation is widespread. It is a basic belief in the Hindu and Buddhist religions. A life force called *karma*, according to these faiths, continues in existence after the end of one earthly span and into another. Usually all memory of the previous life is lost in the transition. The ancient Greeks pictured the spirit after death as drinking of the River Lethe, whose waters dissolved all memory of the past.

Hindus and Buddhists believe that the sum of one's acts in any one earthly life carries over to affect one's status after rebirth. Evil-doing will cause one to have a hard time in the next life; good and noble acts, and doing one's duty, will help one to rise in the next life to a higher plane. Eventually the soul is released, as a reward, from the burdensome cycle of rebirth and joins the Great Universal Spirit in *nirvana*.

According to this belief, occasionally the life force that carries over does not lose all its memory of past lives. This memory, it is thought, is usually buried and comes to the surface only in a trance or under hypnosis. It may happen, though, that while wide awake you visit a place you have known or lived in during a past existence. Suddenly you have a strong sense of recognition, a *déjà vu* experience.

Waking Memories

For example, during World War II as some American troops entered a small Belgian village, one of the soldiers realized that, though he had never been in Belgium before, he knew that village. He knew every shop on the small main street and could lead his platoon straight to an inn and through a house where he knew every room. It seems plausible that he might have lived in that village house during some past life.

Not surprisingly, some of the most amazing reports of reincarnation come from India. There, about fifty years ago, a four-year-old girl kept telling her parents about her past life as a married woman in a city about 100 miles from her home—a place where she had never been. After several years, when she had given her former husband's name and address, her parents wrote a letter to the supposed husband. To their surprise, it developed that there really was such a man at the address their small daughter recalled. When the man's brother came to see them, the child recognized him at once as her brother-in-law and called him by name. And he admitted that his brother had had a young wife who had died in childbirth.

Again, a young Indian boy, just a few years ago, claimed that he remembered his life, marriage and death in a village not far from his home. When his parents took the lad to the village, he recognized a woman as his former wife and reminded her of so many incidents of their

brief life together that she was convinced that the soul of her former husband was indeed housed in this small boy. He also recognized their home and the room that had been his—in which he had died at the age of twenty-one.

These children were not hypnotized or in trance states. They appeared to carry memories of their former lives into everyday hours of their new existences. These reports, which were checked with people still living, are more convincing than former-life memories dredged up under hypnosis or in a trance state. But the fact that these have checked out also makes trance memories more believable.

Trance Recollections

Taylor Caldwell, a noted American authoress, seemed to return under hypnosis to lives her spirit had lived as a woman physician in ancient Greece, as the mother of Mary Magdalen in the Holy Land, as a maid servant in the household of the English author known as George Eliot—and various others. It was impossible to check these long-past existences directly; but evidence supporting the truth of the memories appeared in her novels, which could scarcely have been written by someone who had not had personal experience with the material—for example, with ancient Greek surgical techniques. Under hypnosis she relived a whole operation on a human brain she had done in ancient Greece, lecturing to medical students of the time as she worked. One of her novels was filled with similar information on ancient medical science.

The Swedish playwright and novelist August Strindberg had a different kind of introduction to a life it appeared he had lived long ago. On a visit to the ruins of Pompeii in Italy, he had wandered away from the tour group and drifted through the old streets until evening came. Then, as he rested under an old bridge to escape a sudden rain shower, he heard a spirit call him

by name—a Roman name. And it brought to his mind a long and tangled career he had enjoyed centuries before.

As he made his way back toward the entrance to the ruins, rather shaken by this encounter, an old woman stopped him and led him through the streets to a handsome villa. As they went, he became aware that the city was no longer in ruins and that he himself was dressed in a Roman toga.

When they reached a certain villa, he found himself reunited with a beautiful young woman whom he had loved in Roman times. But their reunion was disturbed by sounds of distant thunder, while the earth beneath them quivered and shook. Rushing out from the villa, they found themselves in the midst of a terrified crowd fleeing the eruption of Mt. Vesuvius.

In the tumult, the lovers were separated, and Strindberg awoke to find himself back in modern times, on the steps of the ruined villa, on the anniversary of the great eruption that had buried Pompeii.

It is not surprising that people who have experienced "far memories" of long-past lifetimes rather frequently write about them.

Taylor Caldwell, whose real name was Joan Grant, insisted that her books were really autobiographies of previous lives she had lived, as a lute player in Italy, an American Indian and a pharaoh in Egypt about the year 3000 B.C.!

In 1938 she relived nursing a woman through smallpox in Italy in 1526. She accurately described the symptoms and each stage of the disease but claimed, contrary to modern medical knowledge, that it included a strong stench. The doctor to whom she told all this was familiar with smallpox. He assured her that there was no

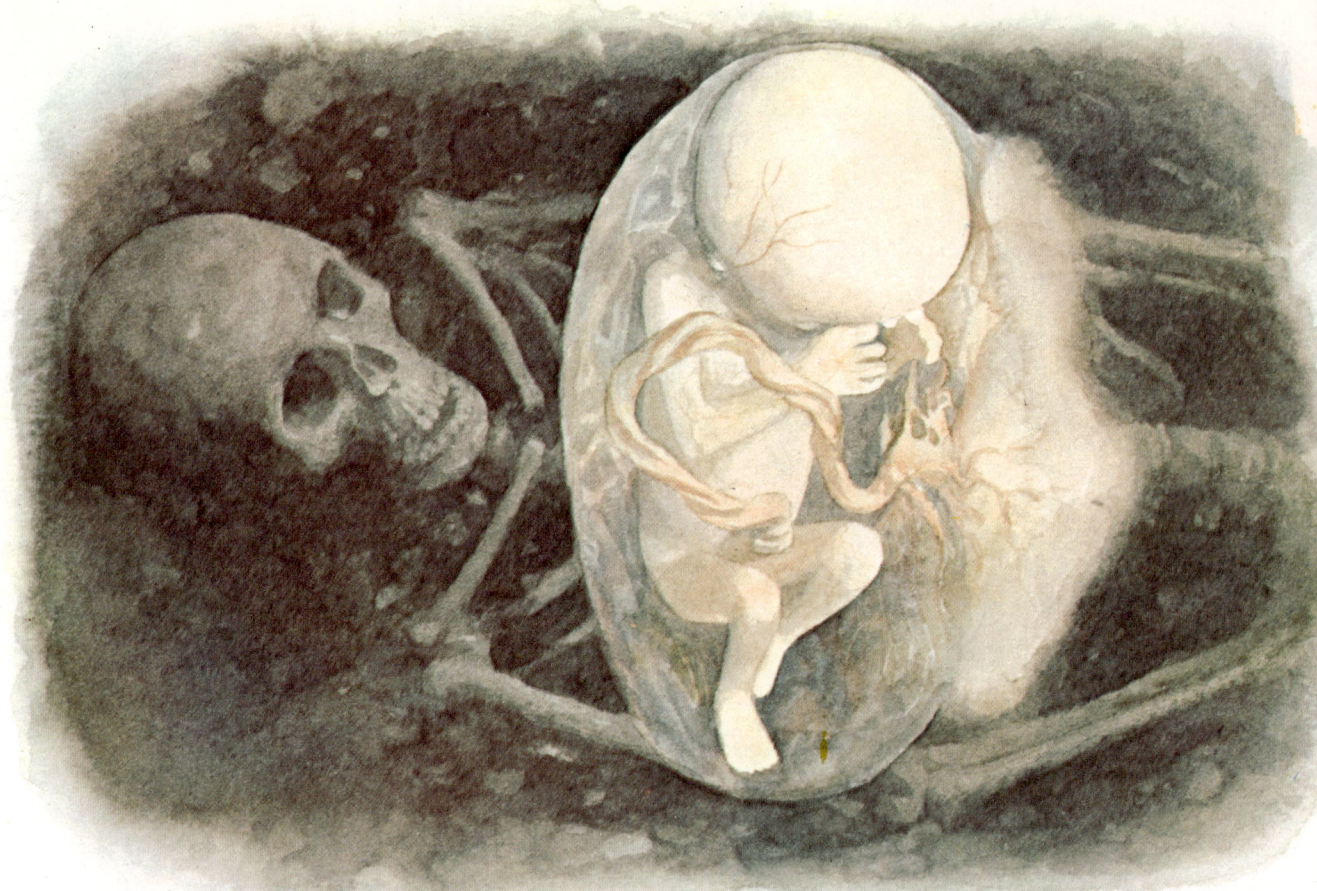

smell associated with it. But some weeks later, scanning a newly arrived medical journal, he came upon an article describing a type of smallpox that had been rampant in Europe during the Middle Ages but was now very rare. One unusual characteristic of this form of the disease was that it was accompanied by a strong stench.

Another case involved a man with very little education and scant knowledge of history who under hypnosis described his life as an English sailor in the sixteenth century. He spoke vividly of a time when he had had scurvy on a long voyage—a common ailment among seagoers in those days. And he described his adventures fighting the Spanish Armada, which he had scarcely heard of when awake.

Various Views

The kind of reincarnation in which some Eskimos and many Africans believe is relatively simple to fathom. They believe that the soul of one who dies reappears in the next baby born to the family or community.

Family resemblances would easily account for the new arrival seeming to be a reincarnation of the well-remembered deceased relative. Vivid recall of past experiences in a faraway and strange land and time are something quite different. One is indeed tempted to credit such recollections to a spirit that lives on and on.

This belief could also account for geniuses, like Mozart, who are almost born with complete mastery of the technique of playing some musical instrument or of composing musical works. It could account for children who babble in strange tongues—babbling which someone recognizes as a foreign language with which the child has (in this life) never had any contact.

Reincarnation might also help explain the fact that in our era of exploding populations, when the world holds so many millions more people than ever before, there seem to be so many who have no sense of belonging, no feeling that they have a place in society. Perhaps they are all new souls, just starting their round of rebirths and unconsciously resentful of the old souls around them whose experiences have roots deep in the dim past.

MYSTERIES SCIENCE CAN'T EXPLAIN

Science has made tremendous advances during the past several decades along a very broad front. But there are still murky areas which prompt many scientists to shrug their shoulders and which challenge others to re-examine orthodox ideas. Here are a few of the widely scattered fields in which knowledge is clouded with mystery.

Seeing Through the Skin

Bestowing the gift of sight to the blind has long been a dream dear to many people. For a few kinds of conditions, marvelous new treatments have been developed. But most blindness eludes cure. Recently scientific research has produced a few experimental models of a rather bulky boxlike device that has raised hopes. Using electrodes attached to the skin, the device enables the surface nerve endings there to substitute for eyes and convey visual messages to the brain. One such device includes a hand-held computer, a lens and a jacket that puts hundreds of electrodes in contact with the skin.

Mass production seems a long way off, and even if it is achieved, the devices are still costly and cumbersome. Meanwhile, a more direct method has been demonstrated and taught successfully. This is skin sight.

Seeing through the skin came to public attention in the early 1960s when a young Russian girl who had worked with the blind in her town found, rather accidentally, that she could see through her fingers.

She was tested over and over again. First she was simply blindfolded. Touching papers of different colors lightly with her fingers, she correctly named the color of each one. As a more difficult test, the colored papers were covered with glass or cellophane, and she was not only blindfolded but seated behind a screen so that only her hands could approach the papers. Even without touching them directly she still managed to tell red from green and yellow from blue. She even went on to read print and musical scores under glass.

Finally scientists in the Soviet Union were willing to admit that this young woman really could see through her skin. (In one demonstration she even read through one elbow.) The next step was to see if this ability could be developed in others.

The first group to try to learn skin sight were some blindfolded art students. When they touched the colored papers they found that different colors had different textures. Yellow was slippery; light blue smooth; red, green and dark blue seemed sticky; orange was rough, violet (strangely) roughest of all.

Seeing at a distance, without touching, proved more difficult, but some of the students mastered it. Then they found that some colors seemed to radiate an electromagnetic force farther than others. The red end of the spectrum (where light rays have the longest wavelength) radiated farthest; the blue (short wavelength) end of the spectrum had the shortest range of radiation.

In addition, the colors seemed to give off heat or cold. Red was hottest, yellow slightly warm, blue tones and violet cool to cold.

With this information in hand, some scientists tried to teach skin seeing to blind children. They found that children learned more readily than blind adults. Some of the youngsters learned to read and identify colors through their skin.

Some scattered work has been done in the United States, France, Bulgaria and other places. One of the few organized teaching programs has been in Bulgaria. There, of a group of sixty blind children, three took to skin sight naturally; but, more importantly, all the other fifty-seven were able to learn it fairly well.

The mechanism in the skin that makes skin sight possible is still a mystery. But it is known that some lower animals do "see" without having what we consider eyes. Jellyfish, corals and worms, for example, "see" by means of groups of pigment cells. These are linked to sensing cells and sometimes are covered with a thickened layer of the outer skin cells called cuticle.

Humans have all these elements in their skin. It is also known that when one sense, such as sight, is lacking in an individual, the remaining ones often develop to an unusual degree. It seems very possible then that the cell combinations that provide some sight to lower animals may be able to work together in certain circumstances to compensate in human beings for a lack of usable eyes. If this is indeed a skill that can be learned, the possibilities for blind people are marvelous.

Hibernation: Possibilities for Space Travel

Travel to the moon and the dispatching of unmanned vehicles to other planets have drawn people's thoughts far out into space. One problem to be faced is the very long time space travelers have to spend in small quarters on the way. This prospect, with complications such as providing food for a long journey, led some to think about hibernation. How much space travel could be simplified if only the travelers could sleep the time away, as bears, ground squirrels, hedgehogs and some other animals sleep through the winter!

Folk tales of olden times in New England claimed that elderly members of a family were sometimes put into a kind of hibernation. Legend has it that they were put into a deep sleep, then wrapped warmly and tucked away, perhaps in a woodshed, for the long winter months. With the approach of spring, they were brought back into the house and allowed to warm up and wake up.

In poor villages of northern Russia, where in pre-Revolutionary times food used to be very scarce during the long winters, whole families

practiced semihibernation, according to authoritative reports. They laid in a good stock of firewood for the stoves in their huts. Most of the family slept on a platform on top of the stove. There they huddled through the months of cold. Now and then one member would rise to poke another log into the stove. Perhaps once a day each member of the family would rouse from sleep to munch a little dry bread. But for the most part they dozed or slept the winter away.

This halfway state would not suffice for space travel, though. What is needed is a true state of hibernation in which breathing, heartbeat and all bodily functions slow almost to the stopping point. Just how this process could be brought on and controlled has puzzled scientists.

What puts animals to sleep when cold weather arrives? And what inner alarm alerts them when the weather turns warm?

One requirement for comfortable hibernation would seem to be a good layer of fat. Animals that have not been able to find a sufficient stock of food in the fall often remain awake, prowling for scarce food through snowy woods or wandering southward in their search. But just having an adequate blanket of fat is not enough to put an animal into a months-long sleep.

Recently scientists took some blood from a hibernating ground squirrel. They made a serum using this blood and injected the serum into a wide-awake squirrel. Promptly the animal fell into a deep slumber, with breathing and heart action slowed as if for a winter's sleep.

This is just a first clue toward the solution of the mystery of hibernation. No one knows what stimulates the production of this chemical that regulates the functioning of the body organs. Nor is it known what time clock readjusts the rate of living in the spring.

Trying out the "hibernation serum" on human beings is a long way off. But once the mystery is solved, astronauts may be given an injection that will permit them to sleep through a long, dull flight to another planet. Upon arrival there, a chemical alarm will awaken them to as yet unheard-of exploration.

Then, with good luck, they may be able to reboard their space craft, reinject themselves and doze off again for the long flight home, thanks to the examples of the hedgehog, bear and ground squirrel.

Dowsing: Strange Power in the Hands

A man holding a forked twig out before him in both hands walks slowly across a field, talking softly to the twig. Occasionally the long straight end of the twig bends down toward the ground, quivering with strange energy. The man is a dowser. When his "rod" bends down, it means to him that there is an underground stream of water below that spot.

Engineers often scoff at the power of dowsers, and it is true that no one knows exactly what the

basis of that power is. But it has worked too often to be ignored.

The use of wizard rods or divining rods, as they are often called, is a very old art. There are records of it in ancient Egyptian and Chinese artwork. The Bible also tells of Moses striking a rock with his staff and water gushing out.

Dowsing works for other things than water. It has been used to locate underground deposits of oil, minerals, even buried treasure.

A dowsing rod need not be a forked twig. Steel rods, coat-hanger wire or a freely swinging pendulum have also been used with success. If a twig is used, it should be freshly cut, as after two or three days the wood is likely to lose its power.

The most important thing is that the rod be in the hands of someone who possesses "the power," whatever that may be!

"Water witches," as those with the power are sometimes called, are usually men over thirty years of age. Generally they are not particularly psychic and work at any of a variety of commonplace occupations.

Some dowsers claim that they have inherited the gift. At least one said his came to him after a tropical fever that made his nervous system more sensitive. It is true that many dowsers report that they feel nausea, dizziness, muscle spasms and tingling of the skin when their rods react to hidden water or other material. Some say they must concentrate on the problem; others make their minds a blank.

People with a highly developed talent for dowsing can tell the depth at which the water—or other material—will be found. In the case of water, they can tell whether or not it will be good to drink as well as direction and force of the flow. An occasional artist with the dowsing rod claims to make it work over a map of an area or even a picture of a site.

Naturally scientists have tried to discover the nature of this power. They have found that a dowser's heartbeat, blood pressure and pulse rate are affected by the mysterious force. They have also discovered, rather surprisingly, that wearing leather gloves kills the action of the force, though rubber or cotton gloves do not.

Some say a dowser's power is mental. Others speculate that it may be related to radioactivity or electromagnetism. Rods do react to magnets—and possibly to the earth's magnetic field. They seem to be affected by weather changes and sometimes even by the angle of the sun.

All these clues are interesting, but so far they have not supplied an answer as to the nature of the unknown force that works through a dowser's sensitive hands.

Rainmaking

Dowsers seem able to find underground waters. Rainmakers claim—and sometimes seem to prove their claims—to be able to make rain fall, more or less at their command.

Back in the early 1900s there was a professional rainmaker named Charles Hatfield at work in the United States. He set up wooden towers wherever he went to work. At the top of each tower was a large wooden tub. This Hatfield filled with chemicals that sent smelly and smoky vapor drifting up to the clouds.

His system seemed quite successful. It brought rains to farms of central California—or seemed to—year after year after year. It apparently helped to put water into the rivers of the Yukon country to help Alaskan miners pan gold. In fact, it was success that ruined Hatfield.

He was hired in 1916 to break a two-year drought in San Diego. He was to be paid by the amount of rain he brought. He put up his towers, installing the chemicals in tubs at the top. Twenty-four hours later the rain began to fall.

Unfortunately Hatfield did not have a formula for turning off the rain, and as days passed San Diego found itself overwhelmed by a disastrous flood. The city fathers refused to pay him, and his suit for his fee was thrown out of court.

Something like Hatfield's system has been accepted by scientists in recent years. Airplanes drop crystals of dry ice into clouds or trail silver iodide smoke through them to cause moisture to condense into drops that fall as rain.

That is relatively easy to understand. But some rainmaking techniques that seem to work are more mysterious.

Folk tales in many parts of the world tell of special ceremonies, chants and dances that make rain fall—or cause the clouds to roll away and the sky to clear. It is easy to turn away from stories like these with a shrug of the shoulders. They can be dismissed as mere fantasy. But what of present-day cases like these?

In 1947 King George VI of England visited Swaziland in South Africa. In preparation for the king's visit, certain sources have reported, the mother of the local chief called for rain to settle the dust. A pleasant shower fell. When the English party arrived she called for sunshine. The clouds at once parted, and the sun shone.

In 1955 a doctor named Rolf Alexander claimed to be able to dissolve clouds by looking at them and willing them to disappear. He was photographed at work, and the photographs do appear to back up reports that he could choose a cloud, concentrate on it and within minutes cause it to vanish. He claimed that charged particles from his body acted on the clouds.

In 1959 a road-building crew unearthed a massive block of soapstone. It had been brought to California by an Indian tribe, and the Indians warned that if the stone remained uncovered rain or snow would fall.

Their warning was not heeded. The stone remained uncovered. The season was warm, but an unprecedented five-inch snowfall was soon recorded there at sea level. The stone was promptly covered!

In 1966 the stone was again uncovered, this time by curious tourists. A flood soon raged over the countryside.

That same year a California professor interested in American Indian cultures became intrigued by the claim of the Zapotec tribe that a clay image of the Indian rain god Cocijo, if placed face up in a field, would scare the heavens into releasing rain. The professor made some of the images and tried them out. He met with surprising success.

Other Indian rainmakers also won fame during the 1960s. During the American Indian Exposition in 1960 the Kiowas, Pueblos and Jemex Indians performed their rainbow and sun dances. Record rainfalls followed. When a forest fire raged in Colorado, Navajos did their rain dance, and rainfall squelched the flames. And during a bad Oklahoma drought, the Apaches did their dance, and abundant rain followed.

Skeptics claim that the unsuccessful dances and other attempts are forgotten and that coincidence accounts for the successes. But does it? Or is there some mysterious power at work along with the drumbeats, the stamping feet and the chanting voices that does rise to and act upon the clouds?

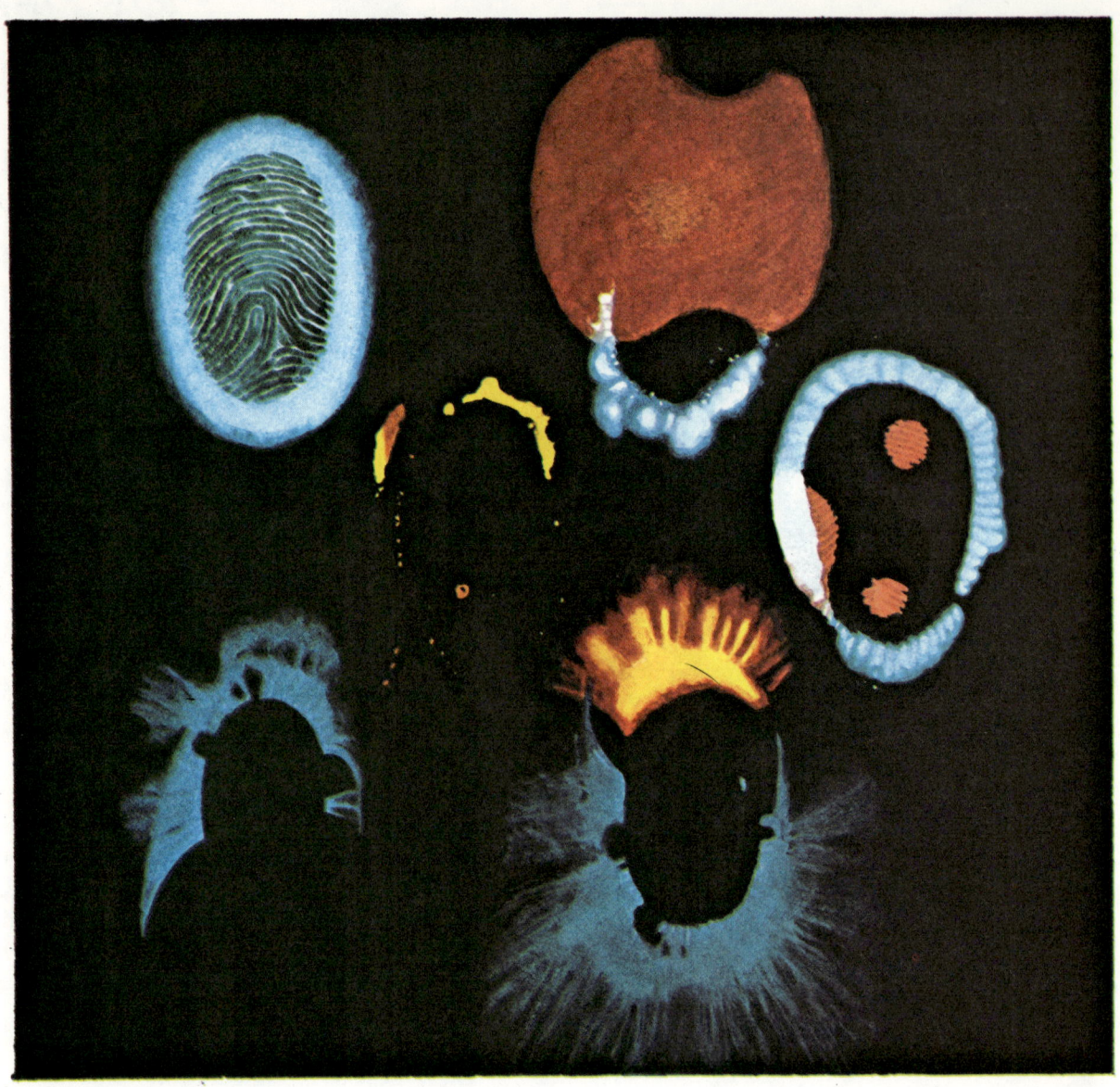

Auras of Many Colors

In a pitch-black room a man places one of his fingertips firmly on the emulsion of a sheet of Polaroid film. An electric spark is sent through both the fingertip and the film—a spark of high voltage, low-wattage electricity.

When the film is developed it shows the oval shape of the fingertip clearly; and all around it extends a pale-blue halo or aura.

Until this system of using photographic film and an electric spark was developed—by a Russian husband-and-wife team named Kirlian—

human auras had been visible mainly to clairvoyants and others with psychic powers.

The aura is an outflowing of force or some weightless, mysterious matter that surrounds all living things with a cloud of light that is usually invisible to human eyes. (For a discussion of the auras of plants, see "Do Plants Have Feelings?")

Old definitions—dating back fifty years or so, when psychic matters were considered superstitions or fakeries by most factually minded

An aura is also often called a nimbus, a Latin word for "cloud." It is a very old and widespread belief that the Christian God and the various gods of other religions live in a heaven beyond the clouds; hence they are pictured as trailing golden "clouds of glory."

In Tibet, where traditionally highly trained lamas claimed to see auras clearly, the golden color was associated with great purity. Those who were "not pure," which would probably include most of us, had pale-blue auras, at least when in a calm, relaxed state. Anger or great tension could make the aura flash out like red flames. A thready or weak aura meant poor health.

Interestingly, this is what the Kirlian photographs also show. If the man whose fingertip was photographed, showing a pale-blue aura, is stirred to hot anger, his same fingertip will photograph with a great flare of scarlet.

A very ill patient whose aura was faint and spotty, with only bits of red and yellow visible on the photographic plate, was observed before and after treatment by a powerful psychic healer. After the treatment some strong red spots remained—but stronger than before—and a "normal" pale blue-white halo surrounded the whole fingertip.

people—spoke of auras as "supposed" forces of weightless matter that proceeded from and surrounded bodies. This weightless substance was supposed to contain the essential nature of the person or other being. And it was thought to be the means through which alleged psychic powers operated.

With the development of more intensive research in parapsychology—the study of experiences beyond physical sciences—and with experimentation in Kirlian photography, which uses techniques of physical science, this skepticism is giving way to respectful acceptance.

The idea of human auras surrounding bodies is a very old one. We see it reflected most often in paintings of saints and of the Holy Family, who are generally shown with rings or halos of pale or golden light around their heads.

deep red
passionate, physical

bright red
aggressive, tense, angry

pink
gentle, dreamy,
self-conscious

orange-brown
skeptical, intelligent,
worldly

gold
highly developed
spiritually

yellow
kindly, wise, noble,
mystical

light green
youthful, hopeful, aspiring

dark green
envious, jealous, hateful

deep blue
psychic, student of occult

light blue
relaxed, kindly, good

violet
earnest, mystical, spiritual

purple
magnetic, successful, just

black
malicious, hateful

The healer was photographed, too, before and after the treatment. Even when she was relaxed, her aura flashed out with unusual streaming brilliance, a deep blue. When her psychic powers were aroused in the course of the treatment, the deep-blue stream flared out even more strikingly than before; but in addition, from the fingertip a sunset glow of gold and orange-red flashed dazzlingly.

Some work was done in the use of auras in diagnosing disease back in the early 1900s. A London doctor discovered that he could see the aura around a human body if he looked through a glass screen stained with certain dyes. And he recorded the changes in auras as they were affected by moods or illness.

Now Kirlian photography promises more help in the direction of early diagnosis of some conditions. For it has been found that traces of ill-health affect the aura before symptoms can otherwise be observed.

If a person's aura disappears completely, death is at hand. It seems that the aura is evidence of the second body, the energy or spirit body, which psychic investigators had speculated that each of us possesses. This spirit body is intertwined with the physical body while a person is alive, and its aura is a reflection of the body's health. As death approaches, the spirit body seems to free itself from its physical home.

The pulsing, glowing color of auras is said to be visible principally to clairvoyants or through the use of high-frequency photography. However, you may be able to get a faint glimpse of your own aura for yourself. Go into a completely dark room and press one hand against a blank wall. You may see a faint, pale glow suggesting the outline of the hand. One religious group that considers auras to be important reflections of the state of an individual's life force has assigned interpretations to the various colors psychically attuned persons may learn to perceive in the auras of others. They believe that certain colors indicate that one's physical, earth-bound self is dominant. Others indicate that the astral, spirit or psychic body dominates an individual's being. Much simplified clues to these interpretations are shown next to the colors in the spectrum at the left.

The Homing Instinct

As the family departs for a new home, there is a sad parting between the children and their pet cat who is being left with neighbors. Weeks later, as the children are becoming accustomed to their new home, they hear a familiar "meow" at the door one day. There, thin and dirty and bedraggled, is their beloved cat.

How did it find its way? "Homing instinct" is the easy answer, but it does not really explain long-distance travels of animals. The cat had never seen the new home, which was across a section of the Alps from the family's old residence. It had no way of following recognized landmarks along the way.

In another instance, an army man was being transferred to another camp, so he sent his cat ahead by train. Within three weeks it found its way across 700 miles of country, back to its old home.

Some people have guessed that in situations like the first one described, the family car might possibly have left a recognizable "scent trail" which the cat followed. But even that does not seem to apply to the second case, nor to hundreds of others.

It does seem to have some relationship to one other story. This is about a family that drove west for a summer vaction, taking with them a six-month-old collie. The family route was a circular one, following a northerly route from Indiana to Oregon, then returning by a more southerly one. Along the way the collie was lost.

The children were very upset, and the parents shared their concern. But there seemed to be nothing to do but to continue the trip.

Six months after the family had returned home the collie reached the family doorstep. Somehow the family was able to trace the dog's route for part of the way he had traveled and found that he had not come back by the highway on which they had traveled west. He too had circled south on his long way home.

The instinct or skill that brings these animals across country to their dear ones is as much a mystery as the related ability of whole flocks of birds, schools of fish and other large groups of animals to migrate hundreds and thousands of miles every year.

It might be assumed that trained leaders guide the flocks of birds across land and sea, following—in the case of wild geese, for example—river valleys and other outstanding features of the land below. But in many bird families, such as the plovers, which fly

thousands of miles, the adults leave the summer homes first. Youngsters stay behind to gain a bit more strength and flying skill. When they start out on the long southward journey, there is no one in the flock who has ever made the trip before.

The same is true of salmon and eels, which swim hundreds of miles through—to us—trackless oceans to spawning grounds. They return to the same areas where they hatched from eggs. But they left those waters when they were very young. And no one makes the return journey twice to show them the way back.

Another possibility that has been suggested is that animals may follow the electromagnetic lines of force that encircle the earth. That might seem to provide an answer for birds—except that they seldom fly straight north or south. Instead, they tend to cluster along broad flyways in the sky. It seems to explain even less about the travel of sea creatures through dark waters.

Scientists have been banding birds and marking young fish for years to try to chart their migrations. They have compiled many, many reports from places along the route where the birds have been seen. But this gives them little clue as to what the power is that led them there.

At least one scientist tried to test the homing instinct by using his own pet cat in a series of experiments. He carried the cat, closed in a bag so it could not see its surroundings, five miles away from his home. Then he released the cat so that it could not see him depart. He went home by a roundabout route. Soon the cat appeared there too.

In further tests the man carried the cat out of town by different routes, to all the points of the compass. Each time the distance home was somewhat longer than before. But the cat always made it back, in times varying from several hours to overnight.

On the last test, the cat was taken sixteen and a half miles from home and released as usual. Its owner went home and prepared to check on its time of arrival. But it never returned. So this scientific experiment leaves us just where we were in our understanding of the homing instinct. It is still a mystery.

Do Plants Have Feelings?

"She has a green thumb." People used to say that admiringly of a woman whose potted plants flourished or whose garden provided particularly lovely blossoms.

"I have a black thumb," a would-be gardener whose plants always seemed to die used to say with a shrug of the shoulders.

No more! Now we hear that the secret lies not in the thumb but in the tongue. Talking sweetly to plants is what causes them to flourish, some people argue currently. Plants may wither, even with proper sunlight, regular watering and careful feeding, unless they have thoughtful and attentive care.

A group of high-school students checked this theory with rows of bean plants. They showed affection to one row, indifference to a second and hatred to a third. The first row flourished, the second languished and the third actually died.

Plants seem to respond to music as well as to attention in the form of the human voice. Fields of corn and wheat that were serenaded with music gave remarkably high yields. It has been reported, moreover, that the kind of music matters. Some plants do very well when Beethoven or other classical music is played nearby. But leaves actually curl up or stalks lean away from the sound when rock music is heard.

In some cases plants respond to unspoken thoughts or to psychic suggestion. When one experimenter thought about cutting down or tearing up a plant, even though he said nothing, the plant seemed to quiver as if with fear. The prospect of violence seemed to have as much effect—negatively—as affectionate words did positively. One strongly psychic person showed that he could influence the growth of plants just by passing his hand over them.

A fascinating series of experiments was undertaken under the guidance of a Protestant minister. It involved the sprouting of seeds. Two sets were started under identical conditions except for the fact that prayer was directed to one set.

In one experiment, in each of two pans filled with identical earth, eight kernels of corn were

planted. Two more pans were planted with lima beans, a third set with sweet peas. The pans were kept side by side, in the same temperature, with the same amount of sunlight. But the jar of water from which one half of the pans were watered had been prayed over by each member of a group. The other jar contained the same kind of water but had received no prayer.

Seven of the prayed-over corn kernels grew, while only three of those not prayed over did. Four of the prayed-four lima beans grew; none in the other pan grew. Only one of the prayed-over sweet peas grew, to three of the not-prayed-for. Even prayer did not achieve perfect success. But in this and many following experiments, it made an impressive difference. It was even discovered that prayers to halt growth—like scorn replacing love—could cause leaves to wither and stems to droop.

What is the meaning of all this? To skeptics it sounds like nonsense, but firm evidence is piling up. Surely a plant cannot understand English—or any other spoken language. Surely it cannot actually hear or read a mind.

The answer seems to be that every living thing is surrounded by an energy field, a form of energy as yet not identified or measured by science. These energy fields are affected by changing emotions or states of health. Some "wavelengths" in the fields mesh or balance well; others work at counter-purposes. A plant responds—through its energy field—to other

fields around it. It reacts to the effects on these fields of emotions or illness or even death.

Fruits, vegetables, eggs—even simple amoebas and bacteria—have energy fields, it seems, through which they can react. One doctor connected fruits and vegetables to an electrical machine and "heard" their reactions as they were peeled, sliced and bitten.

Who's Guilty?

Scientists interested in the sensitivity of plants have attached polygraphs to them. Our most frequent association with polygraphs is through their use as "lie detectors." Basically what they do is measure—in the form of a graph—changes in physical reactions.

When one polygraph expert, as a test, thought about burning a leaf, the pen of the polygraph attached to the plant "almost shot off the paper," the plant's reaction was so violent.

Some plants seem to have sensitivity as intense as that of a psychic person. One experimenter connected his plants to polygraphs, machines that record changes in bodily functioning. Then he went off for an evening's entertainment. When he returned and checked the graphs he found that at least one plant had undergone changes that paralleled his own changing moods during the evening, even though he was miles away.

In another test plants wired to polygraphs were carried along a police line-up. Among the several men was one murderer. The plants responded quite differently when they came close to the murderer and his energy field.

Plants have also been moved over the body of a sick person, and the polygraph has shown that they respond differently to the area of the body where the problem lies than to any other part of the person. This suggests that plants may prove helpful in diagnosing ailments in humans.

A Glow of Light

Since the outpourings of energy from human beings in the form of auras have been photographed, it seemed natural to try photographing the auras of plants. The experiment worked. A pattern of small round flares appeared scattered over and around the image of a healthy leaf or bud.

Some buds that showed bright halos were cut in half and rephotographed with a high-frequency current. The plumes of light poured out more brightly, with a special glow in the center of the slashed bud. When the buds were cut off entirely, a gush of energy poured from the damaged plant—as energy has been seen to pour out (in the form of an aura) from the fingertips of overfatigued people.

As work with plant auras continued, some strange phenomena appeared. If a piece were torn out of a leaf, its aura might still be complete. This suggested that plants may have double natures—one physical, the other an astral or energy being—just as some people feel is true of human beings.

As with human beings, there is evidence that the aura of a plant or leaf responds more quickly to disease than the physical being. When a leaf that seemed healthy showed a very weak aura, the plant it came from proved to have been infected with a fatal disease. But neither the leaf nor the plant showed any physical symptoms of disease when the aura appeared weak.

Perhaps the most fantastic experiment involved wiring a plant to electrodes attached to a man. To the man's amazement, he felt the life of the plant moving through his body. He felt the rush of water up the stem, carrying nourishment from the soil to the leaves. He experienced the sensation of the sunlight as it touched leaf surfaces, setting in motion the process of photosynthesis.

This man was no psychic. He was a down-to-earth scientist. His reaction to the sensing of the life processes within a plant opens up a whole new possible field of research—a field as yet uncharted and mysterious.

Snake Charmers

The wistful, haunting notes of flutelike music drifts in through your window. If that window faces a street in a town in India the chances are good that a snake charmer is at the gate. In front of him there is sure to be a sizable basket, and it is at this basket that he directs his attention as he tootles a mournful air.

Now watch the basket closely. Slowly the broad head of a cobra, with its flaring hood, appears. As the serpent uncoils its sinuous length, its head rises to the level of the charmer's pipe, weaving back and forth as if in time to the music.

"How can this be?" you may ask. "Aren't snakes deaf?"

Some people think that it is the vibration of the sound waves that excites the snake. Others have observed that the snake often emerges from its basket only when tapped. They think that the swaying of the snake as it follows the movement of the charmer's pipe is part of the serpent's effort to come close enough to lash out with its poison fangs. But that is too simple an explanation to fit the facts.

In India, and in some other tropical lands from the Philippines to Africa, poisonous snakes are a real menace to village life. Snake charmers perform a service, not just in piping their own snakes but in luring wild snakes from hiding.

The snake charmer's tools are his reed pipe, a forked stick and a burlap bag. He pipes on his reed, with puffed-out cheeks, until the snake appears from hiding. Then he stabs at the snake

with his stick—sometimes pinning its head down firmly with the forked end of the weapon so he can safely pick the snake up—and he slides its six-foot length into the burlap bag.

This considerate handling is possible with the Indian cobra, which generally does not grow to be more than six feet long. In India, where the Hindu and Buddhist religions oppose the killing of snakes or any form of life, it is considered proper to treat the snake gently. The deadly king cobra, which often grows to between twelve and eighteen feet in length and holds enough venom in its poison glands to kill an elephant, is usually not treated so gently. It is found mainly in Southeast Asia, from Burma and Malaysia to the Philippines.

Some snake charmers attract snakes with whistling instead of piping. Others use drums, chants or an imitation of the serpents' hissing mating call. A few have even been known to dominate the great snakes by the force of their glance or personality. This suggests that snake charming may be a form of hypnotism.

Whatever the mysterious power may be, it has been observed too often to be doubted. Women snake charmers sometimes specialize in the "Kiss of Death," in which they climax their performance by touching their lips to the head of the charmed snake—often a king cobra.

Unfortunately, though, the snake charmer's power, like most psychic forces, is not wholly reliable; it seems to ebb occasionally. Few snake charmers, it has been noted, live to enjoy even middle age. They die of snakebites.

The Power to Heal

Doctors are willing to admit that the mind plays an important part in healing. Many forms of ill-health can be caused or worsened by worry or depression. Many illnesses that have physical causes can still be influenced by the attitude of the sufferer. But doctors are baffled by examples of mental healing and faith healing.

Sleep Healing

On a couch a slightly built man lay asleep. Beside him a friend said quietly, "We have here a child, a five-year-old girl. You will go over her body and tell us the cause of her retardation."

From his trance the man on the couch began to speak. "The trouble is in the spine," he said. He recounted the incident that had caused the misalignment of some vertebrae—a fall the child's parents had all but forgotten and had disregarded at the time. Then he described the adjustments that would correct the condition.

All this was done while the child was in her own home, some miles away from the sleeping psychic. But when the small girl's spine was checked, the vertebrae were found to be in just the condition he had described. And the treatment he prescribed soon returned her to health.

The man was Edgar Cayce, one of America's most famous psychic healers. He had dropped out of school in the sixth grade and had no further formal education. But in his trances he used complex medical terminology which, when he was awake, meant nothing to him.

From 1901 to 1944, he provided through his trances more than 15,000 diagnoses for patients, most of whom he never saw. He also prescribed treatments and medications; some were simple changes in diet, exercises or herbal massages. Others were compounds so complicated that they amazed druggists asked to prepare them. But they worked. And he ordered some of the treatments years before teams of scientists developed the same solutions to the same problems!

Many of Edgar Cayce's prescriptions are still being followed. But the source of his psychic knowledge is still a mystery.

A Healing Team

When two psychics meet and marry, something unusual might well be expected. This was the case with a couple who lived an outwardly normal life for many years near Baltimore.

The unusual part of their life was their mental—or spiritual—healing. Both had had psychic experiences that might be called typical: They had seen spirits of dead people or had had premonitions of death that proved to be accurate. They had "sensed" experiences connected with objects they touched. But the thing that molded both their lives as adults was that they discovered that they had in their hands the power to heal actual, physical conditions.

It seemed that the important thing was to relax so that the healer's life force was on the same wavelength as that of the patient. Then as the healer put his—or her—hands quietly on the patient's back, shoulder, knee or other affected part—perhaps massaging it lightly—the pain went out of it. That might be credited to hypnotism or the power of suggestion. But in addition, swelling went down. Lumpy growths disappeared permanently. Heart and lung conditions that had threatened death vanished and never recurred.

This couple, Ambrose and Olga Worrall, never did their healing as a profession. The husband worked as an engineer to support the household. They did not accept money for their treatments. Nor did they scorn medical science. They insisted that people who came to them consult doctors and use medical science as far as it could help them. They were themselves Christians and believed that their power was God-given, but they did not insist that their patients pray with them or accept any religious beliefs.

The husband described his technique as "the laying on of hands, the certainty of God's love as revealed in the patient, awareness of healing forces within myself and the patient, awareness of currents that flow without conscious effort on my part."

Their cures were not always instantaneous; often long periods of treatment were needed to bring gradual improvement. Sometimes healing did not come at all. The healers frankly did not know what made the difference between their successes and failures. Often, however, doctors who had been treating their patients told them, "I don't know what it is, but keep right on doing it because it is a miracle."

Healthy Soul, Healthy Body

"If you believe that I, as an individual, have any power to heal, you are dead wrong," says one evangelist whose church services and broadcast programs have become famous as a source of miraculous cures. "I have had nothing to do with . . . any healing that has taken place in any physical body. . . . All I can do is point you to the . . . Great Physician, and I can pray; but the rest is left with you and God."

She reminds her audiences of the miracles Jesus performed, many of them done without touching the sufferer. The blind were made to see, the lame to walk, the sick were cured, and evil spirits were driven out of the possessed.

Many of the evangelist's cures have been attested to by surgeons and other medical men who had given up on the patients as hopeless.

One woman had cancer that spread throughout her vital organs. Her family sent prayer requests to the evangelist's services, but the woman continued to become weaker and her pain mounted. After some weeks her family took her in great discomfort to a service, practically carrying her into the hall. On the way home she said she was hungry and ate a good meal—her first in months.

The family continued to join in prayer for help; and within a few months the woman who had been at death's door was strong and well. Several years later, when she needed relatively minor surgery, the doctors were amazed to find that all the once cancer-ridden organs were perfectly sound.

A man whose legs had been paralyzed for years by a war injury and who had had forty-one surgical operations stood up and walked during one of the preacher's services, throwing away his crutches.

A woman suffering from the advanced stage of multiple sclerosis in which both hands and feet were useless began to listen to the evangelist's broadcasts. Some days later, she suddenly began to shake "as if she would fall apart." Then the shaking stopped, and feeling flowed back into her arms, legs, hands and feet. She had to learn to walk again but soon was restored to perfect health.

The evangelist credits all her miraculous cures to faith in God, though many of the people had not been concerned about religion before their cures. Other religious healers agree that the spirit of God moves through them—with a touch of their hands or even at a distance—to cure the sick.

Miracles at Lourdes

In 1858 a young French peasant girl named Bernadette Soubirous reported that the Virgin Mary had appeared before her in a grotto near her home. At first she was not taken seriously, but as she kept reporting conversations with the Virgin, people began to believe her. Soon the rumor spread that a certain spring bubbling from the rocky countryside where Bernadette had scratched at the ground had miraculous power to heal. As evidence of the spring's powers piled up, the Catholic Church declared that the visions were true, and a shrine grew up around the spring at Lourdes, to which more and more pilgrims came in hope of help for their ailments.

Scornful skepticism toward Bernadette's experience turned to acceptance, then to reverence. And fifty-four years after her death she was made a saint of the church.

Thousands of people visit the shrine every year. Not all are helped physically. But some say they experience a sensation like an electrical current passing through them. Others feel a "sweep of waves" or hands upon them. There have been thousands of cases of remarkable improvement or cures. All are checked so carefully by a medical bureau that between 1914 and 1955 only 262 were certified by the bureau. These were then passed on to the Church authorities, and after the most thorough study, some fifty-four have been declared miracles.

One of these miracles cured a young Austrian woman hopelessly confined to bed and wheel chair with an incurable kidney and glandular ailment. In 1950 she prevailed upon her mother to accompany her to Lourdes. There the medical examiner ordered her to plunge into the icy pool below Bernadette's spring.

Trembling and shaking from the icy cold of the water, she thought she must be dying. But as she stepped from the water, she felt not only

refreshed and lively but hungry. She, who for years had to be fed lying down, sat in the hotel dining room with her mother and ate a full meal with relish.

Returning to Vienna, she was able to undergo training and enter a new vocation—machine knitting—at which she could earn her own living. And five years after her cure, following the most strenuous and skeptical investigation, it was officially declared a miracle.

The Danger

Religious leaders say that spiritual transformations usually accompany these amazing cures. Skeptics claim that a change in attitude and concentration of mental energy may be responsible for some of the cures.

One important point is that leading mental healers have usually worked with the medical profession. They have not scorned sensible medical or surgical procedures. Nor have they promised certain cures themselves.

As with psychic mediums, whose successes led to a good deal of fakery for profit, so mental healing has attracted its share of charlatans. They may take advantage of the despair of those deemed hopelessly ill or the fear of others faced with surgery. Promising painless healing, they may defraud patients of large sums of money. Worse still, they may keep people from getting proper medical help that could benefit them.

The power to heal—or to act as a channel for the healing power of God—is a great and mysterious gift. But it is also a very rare one.

Strange Flames

A woman lay on a hospital operating table, prepared for abdominal surgery. As the surgeon made the first incision there was a sharp sound, and a mass of blue flame hovered low above the opened abdomen for several minutes.

The staff in attendance was naturally amazed. But this was not incomprehensible, since the woman's condition was one likely to cause gas to impact under pressure. With the sudden addition of oxygen, the gas ignited.

About the same time, a priest went to consult his physician about an embarrassing and troubling occurrence. Whenever he approached the candles on the altar in the course of his service, his exhaled breath burst into flame.

Again, while this was highly unusual, it could be explained in terms of gases produced in connection with the digestive process.

A more mysterious case apparently of human spontaneous combustion occurred more than twenty years ago in Florida. Publicity surrounding the incident brought out rumors and hints of other bizarre blazes that seemed to fall into the same general category. But this one at least is a matter of record.

An elderly woman who lived alone had had two visitors one evening—her son and a long-time friend. Both reported that they had left her in good spirits, seated in her favorite armchair and smoking a cigarette. Next morning the friend returned to find the armchair and its occupant completely consumed by fire. All that was left of them was a small heap of embers. Among the embers were found a few charred bones, bits of steel spring and a weirdly shrunken skull! Most surprising of all, the fire had touched nothing else in the small, crowded room.

After lengthy study, the police decided to list the death as having been caused by falling asleep while smoking. That was a simple explanation, but it did not fit the facts. A cigarette could not have started a fire hot enough to consume the body and chair so completely without spreading to the rest of the room. And no fire from any known source would have the power to shrink a human skull to the size of an orange, as had happened in this instance.

Some authorities speculate that an absence of a part of Vitamin B complex called inositol might create an imbalance of phosgene, which resembles nitroglycerin. This compound is known to accumulate in people who get little physical exercise. The theory is that overdressing or sitting in an overheated room, as many elderly people like to do, would cause perspiration. And the sweat might act as a "match," causing the body to burn, in the words of the report, "like wet gunpowder."

This is just a theory. Looking at that shrunken skull, at the unburned draperies at the nearby window, at the room with little smoke damage, then at the small heap of ash, insurance investigators shook their heads and chalked the fire up as a mystery.

Unidentified Flying Objects

The time was October 1973; the place, the Florida Gulf Coast. Two fishermen were spending a quiet evening on a deserted stretch of riverbank.

As the darkness deepened, a luminous blue blob appeared in the sky, dipped, circled, hovered and then landed. From an opening in the side of the roughly oblong vehicle floated three figures, pale against the glow.

As the two fishermen—a forty-five-year-old man and a nineteen-year-old youth—watched transfixed, the figures approached them. Paralyzed by fear, shock or some unknown force, the two felt themselves float into the craft. Once inside, a big eyelike instrument studied them as they were turned slowly around. After this careful scrutiny they were put back on the pier where they had been quietly fishing.

The younger man said later that he had blacked out when the figures approached him. He had to be hospitalized for a complete physical and emotional breakdown. The older man, though he suspected that he would be laughed at, decided he must tell their story "so government officials would know of it."

He was surprised, he admitted some months later, by the number of people who were willing to accept his report. The sheriff's department of the county decided that the two were clearly telling the truth as they knew it; but as the older of the two men put it, "I always feel there's something important I can't remember, no matter how hard I try."

The U.S. government was not much interested. The Air Force abandoned its twenty-year study of unidentified flying objects several years earlier, saying it was "inconclusive." It had compiled 10,000 reports of sighting.

Many could be explained as reflections of the sun or moon on ice crystals in clouds, or as birds, kites, advertising blimps, airplanes or weather balloons. But the Air Force admitted that five or six percent were mysteries. This is more than 500 sightings, many by pilots, radar men, policemen—and astronauts. And some of the reports are very hard to explain away.

Way Back When

Published reports of strange flying objects began to appear before the first airplane left the ground. In 1873 a shiny object dived down from Texas skies, panicking a team of horses and frightening a group of farm workers. In 1885 a glowing cigar-shaped craft was reported over Turkey. In 1887 another was seen over Nova Scotia.

In the early months of 1897 separate reports of sightings came from Kansas, Missouri, Nebraska, Colorado, many points in Texas and West Virginia and in Chicago. Some of these "glowing cigar-shaped objects" (as most of them were described) were seen by thousands of people, according to newspaper articles of the time.

The craft seen in Kansas landed on the farm of a sober, reliable and trustworthy man. He said that it was about 300 feet long and that several figures appeared from the carriage below the "cigar" and roped one of his heifers, which was carried off in the ship.

In 1908 a huge unidentified object exploded in the sky above Siberia and crashed in a great ball of flame that sent up a mushroom-shaped cloud and flattened trees for miles around. It also left radioactivity in the area that was still measurable fifty years later. And old inhabitants recalled that people of the countryside died afterward of a strange sickness. Could it have been a nuclear-powered spaceship that crashed? In 1908? And if so, where did it come from?

More Recent Events

In 1946 many people in Scandinavia and nearby sections of Russia saw luminous objects moving across the sky with darting motions, changing speed and direction more suddenly than any man-made craft could do.

In 1947 a dozen passengers and crew members of a steamship traveling off East Africa saw a strange, long, metallic aircraft that paced their ship for some minutes before darting away.

In 1950 an airline pilot and co-pilot radioed to the control tower in Washington, D. C., that a big

On rare occasions, for example once in 1955 when an astronomer and his wife were crossing the United States by train, both of the two different kinds were sighted flying together. The astronomer estimated the long ship as being about 800 feet in length, the round one as about 100 feet in diameter.

Several other astronomers have reported seeing unidentifiable flying objects through the lenses of their telescopes. One of the earliest of these sightings was in England in 1882; another followed in Mexico in 1883.

Spacemen's Views

Other sightings by astronomers have been reported in recent years. But more pertinent are the records of American astronauts and Russian cosmonauts. These men are not only highly intelligent, highly trained and well balanced; they also have the advantage of a totally new viewpoint—from out in space.

The first American space traveler, John Glenn, reported in 1962 that three objects fol-

dark object that glittered faintly in the moonlight appeared first ahead of their plane, then to the left, next to the right. Finally it shot out in front of the airliner and vanished.

Radar men in Washington also spotted the object and confirmed that it was not a plane. But what was it? No one knows.

In 1957 two civilians in West Texas reported that their truck had been stopped by a glowing object that swooped down and landed on the highway in front of them. Its light was so bright that it blinded them for the moment so they could not see any more detail. That same night, while responding to one of several calls reporting similar sightings, four police officers saw the same thing.

Most viewers have reported the unidentified flying objects as fitting one of two descriptions: They were long, cigar-shaped, resembling dirigibles (except that dirigibles are slow-moving), or they were disc-shaped with low domes on top. This is the shape that gave rise to the name "flying saucer."

lowed and overtook him. In the years since, twenty or more spacemen—both American and Russian—including the Skylab crews of the early 1970s, have reported not only seeing but photographing strange flying objects.

Sometimes the unidentified space vehicles just flashed past the Russian or American capsules. Other times they seemed to be observing them closely or following, even chasing them. Most of the space vehicles were reported to be disc-shaped, but some were said to be cylinders or egg-shaped structures.

In Ancient Times

Some believers in the occult—or the supernatural—are reminded by these reports of flying objects of tales handed down from ancient times. In very old Indian writings there are accounts of flying machines built of wood, with metal interiors and two widely spread wings. They reportedly traveled through the air but had fire within them. Often these machines are associated in the stories with gods who live in the skies. Sometimes beings from space are referred to. One story has a stranger appear who agrees to build a flying chariot at the request of the queen.

India's great epic poem, the *Ramayana*, often mentions flying machines. Like the *Iliad* and *Odyssey* of ancient Greece, the *Ramayana* tells of a legendary romance that led to cataclysmic warfare. But whereas in the *Iliad* and *Odyssey* travel was by sailing ship or horse-drawn chariot, in the *Ramayana* much of the travel and some of the fighting took place in the air and involved huge, two-story, beautifully decorated flying boats.

People who believe in visitors to earth from outer space remind skeptics that a hundred years ago the *Iliad* and *Odyssey* were thought to be simply tales made up by master minstrels. It was only when archaeologists who treated the poems as history searched for and found many of the cities and other places described in the epics that people realized that there was a solid basis of history behind the adventures.

Still the dubious battle lasted
Until Rama in his ire,
Wielded Brahma's deathful weapon,
Flaming with celestial fire.

Perhaps the same is true of the *Ramayana* and other Indian classics in which flying machines and weapons that sound like rockets, bombs and nuclear-powered devices are common. Isn't it possible that some of the giants, angels and gods who walked among men in the old tales were really visitors from outer space? They may occasionally have shared their knowledge of how to build flying chariots with earthly folk.

Not all these references are to be found in Indian literature. There are also some in very old Egyptian writings. And in the Old Testament Jacob—presumably in a dream—sees "a ladder set up on earth, and the top of it reached to heaven; and behold, the angels of God were ascending and descending on it." Again in the Old Testament the prophet Elijah is swept up into heaven in a "chariot of fire." Is it possible that these referred to marvels dimly remembered by storytellers from the long-ago past?

To some people it seems reasonable to believe that beings from other planets have been keeping watch over us on earth through long ages. Tales of a thousand years ago also tell of "demon ships" seen in the skies.

One Irish church of the tenth century was reported to have an anchor caught in its roof as a memento of a visit by a flying ship that dropped anchor there during a Sunday mass. Unfortunately the sailors of the skies were apparently frightened by the appearance of the priest and his congregation outside the church. The visitors cut their anchor rope and hastily soared —or sailed—away.

Landings

Landings of flying crafts from other worlds have been reported from many parts of the globe. In Australia in 1966 a group of high-school teachers saw the landings and photographed one of the three circular landing spots where reeds were crushed in an area thirty feet across.

A number of years before that incident some Australian aborigines—who had never heard of "flying saucers" and so could not have been influenced by what they had read—reported seeing a round object land. As they watched from a distant hilltop, they saw that another similar vehicle had already landed. Then they saw a small figure, something like a human being but considerably smaller, transfer from one vehicle to the other. Soon after that both vehicles—which they described as being much like those seen in 1966 by the teachers—took off into the sky.

Space Travelers

The occupants of these mysterious vehicles have been seen on a number of scattered occasions and by reputable people. Interestingly, all the reports agree quite closely. This is especially impressive since the reports come from Mexico, Germany, New Guinea and Venezuela as well as the United States and Australia.

All who have seen the "space travelers" agree that they are about three and a half feet tall. Most viewers report that the strangers were dressed in shiny suits apparently of some metallic material and that they wore helmets. Only once, in Venezuela, were the little people spotted without their metallic coverings, and then they were described as hairy.

The spacemen's visit to Venezuela apparently lasted over several weeks, as several separate encounters were reported. And in each case the human beings came out of the encounters badly scratched or slashed and in a state of shock.

To make these stories more believable, the hospitals where the men and boys in Venezuela were treated reported that the patients had definitely not been drinking. And several of the sightings have been attested to by well-known doctors, teachers, ministers, university students and others who would be unlikely to believe in superstitions.

In addition to the sightings of ships and crews, there have been reports of power failures in some communities at the same time the UFOs were sighted. And since the earliest days of radio broadcasting, there have been reports of radio beep patterns being mysteriously returned minutes after the pattern had been sent out.

There seems no reason to doubt the honesty of many of the reporters. What, then, are the flying objects? Are they really spaceships? If so, where are the small visitors from? Are they trying to communicate with us on earth by sending back our own radio messages—the only language they can feel sure we will understand?

Evidently they do not mean us any harm. There is no record of any violence connected with their visits beyond the attacks on a few people in Venezuela who unintentionally came too close. These attacks represent nothing more than the kind of lashing out in self-defense we would be likely to try if we were exploring a strange world and stumbled upon creatures much larger than ourselves. The power failures associated with sightings were very likely accidental side effects of their approach with unknown power systems—if the sightings were indeed space craft.

If not, what were they?

One cannot help wondering where the next act of this strange play will be staged, where the next chapter of the story will be written. Who will be the first human being to establish friendly contact with the visitors? Or will there instead be a new explanation to account for these mysterious objects of the skies? Perhaps the coming years will reveal the answer.

WITCHCRAFT, SORCERY AND THE OCCULT

"Double, double, toil and trouble; Fire burn and cauldron bubble," recites the famous witch of Shakespeare's Macbeth. Witches and ghosts sometimes appear in Shakespeare's plays, a dramatic device reflecting the sixteenth century's widespread belief in the art of black magic. Today witchcraft is little more than popular folklore celebrated on Halloween. Small sects of self-proclaimed witches and wizards still flourish, though, and other practices of the occult such as fortunetelling enjoy a large following—demonstrating that many people continue to believe in magical prophecy and power.

What Is Witchcraft?

Witchcraft involves supernatural powers. Unlike some other supernatural powers, however, those involved in witchcraft are commonly thought to be for evil-doing. These can include the ability to take the form of various animals, to turn milk sour or to make people ill. But witches can also have powers for good; they can find and remove the cause of illness, read people's minds and make them love or hate at the will of the witch.

The words "witch" and "wicked" come from the same root, and even though witches can be agents for good, most witches are considered wicked. Their supernatural talent is thought to come from black magic, from making a bargain with the devil.

Witches, Wizards and Warlocks

Witches have always been assumed to be women. Men with similar supernatural powers have been known as wizards—"wise ones"—or warlocks or sorcerers.

Merlin was perhaps the most famous wizard. According to many stories, he lived at the court of King Arthur of the Round Table. Merlin could see the future as clearly as the past, could turn people into animals and back at will and had all sorts of supernatural powers which he used for good rather than evil.

Warlocks in general have been thought to use their powers for evil. They have been principally concerned with casting spells and forecasting the future. These skills will be discussed in the next chapter.

Long-ago Witches

Witchcraft has roots deep in history. Nearly 4,000 years ago King Hammurabi of Babylonia had the earliest set of written laws we know of carved into stone. And one of these laws was against the practice of witchcraft.

References to witches also appear in ancient Egyptian writings and some of the books of the Bible. The most famous witch in the Bible was a woman of Endor whom King Saul of the Israelites went by moonlight to consult. She was known to have a "familiar spirit." A witch's "familiar" may take the form of an animal such as a black cat or it may be an invisible spirit. With the help of her spirit, the witch of Endor called up from the afterworld the ghost of Samuel the prophet. And he truly foretold King Saul's death in the battle to come.

The Spirits of the Dead

The calling up of spirits of the dead used to be known as necromancy. In modern times people who claim to be able to communicate with spirits of the dead are called mediums. They are considered to be intermediaries between the worlds of the living and the dead. They do not consider themselves to be witches, and others do not consider them so. They are not thought to have evil powers.

The Ways of Witches

In the Middle Ages it was widely believed that witches were organized in groups called covens. They were thought to meet regularly to plan their mischief and to practice their strange rites and skills.

Witches were generally thought to be able to change their form, often transforming themselves into the animal shape of their "familiars." For many hundreds of years it was also widely accepted that they could fly through the air. And it was whispered that they killed and ate small children or handsome young men, or that they stole people's hearts to eat, replacing the warm hearts with blocks of unfeeling wood.

The idea of participating in these supernatural powers and blood-tingling adventures apparently appealed to many young people in those days. Young women, even children, were often enticed or lured into joining a coven.

Their initiation took place at one of the great conventions held several times a year by the witches and sorcerers for the celebration of their unholy Black Sabbath, also called Witches' Sabbath. This ceremony, a bizarre midnight revelry, was presided over, it was said, by the devil himself.

One of the favorite spots for these gatherings was a peak in Germany's Harz Mountains, long a center of paganism within the Christian world. Halloween, which preceded the Christian All Saints' Day, was one of the several nights during which the witches celebrated.

Another gathering night for witches was Midsummer's Eve. In Scandinavia, great bonfires are still lit to blaze through the brief hours of this pale summer night. Today these bonfires are taken no more seriously than our jack-o-lanterns on Halloween. But in olden days they were seriously meant to drive away witches.

Jack-o-lanterns, incidentally, originally rep-

resented skulls. They were placed in windows on nights when witches flew to indicate friendliness toward them. This was supposed to keep a household safe from their mischief.

The Black Sabbath

In preparation for the Black Sabbath, witches stripped and were rubbed with a special ointment. Then, mounted on long, two-pronged sticks or, later, on broomsticks, they departed by way of the chimney, often accompanied by a goat.

Some witches were pictured with cloth attached to their broom handles, sail fashion, so that the wind could speed them on their way. Others fastened lighted candles to the twigs of their brooms to illuminate their paths. The sight of these small lights flickering across the sky was supposed to alert people down below to what was going on.

There was tremendous interest in and curiosity about witchcraft in the Middle Ages. Apparently some people who were themselves not witches or sorcerers somehow got permission to attend the unholy rites as observers.

It is difficult for us, so far removed from medieval times, to judge the accounts of the witches' celebrations. Most of us are inclined just to be amused at reports of throngs of women, young and old, stripped and greased, riding through the sky on broomsticks. Just how much truth and how much fantasy is contained in accounts of the goings-on at Witches' Sabbaths is impossible to tell. But there seems to have been some basis in fact for all the stories.

One explanation is that the ointment rubbed on the bodies of the witches was a substance that drugged them so that they only felt as though they had been flying and otherwise amusing themselves. Whatever the truth of the matter, hundreds and thousands of people in many lands were involved. And enough real harm was

done in witchcraft so that kings issued decrees condemning it.

Witches' Brews

Witchcraft was associated with the worship of pre-Christian gods. It was thus considered anti-Christian at a time when Christianity was the legal state religion in almost every country in Europe.

According to accounts, the Black Mass celebrated at Witches' Sabbaths did directly mock Christian worship. So witches and warlocks were hunted down as wicked and depraved creatures who could cause great harm. And untold numbers of men and women were burned alive for reportedly practicing witchcraft.

In many European villages it is still believed that there are sorcerers and witches about, casting evil spells. Using their talismans—bells, dice, small skulls and broken crosses thought to have powerful magic effects—and chanting certain charms, they still, it is assumed, concoct weird potions. Some of the simpler ingredients allegedly ground and stirred in their cauldrons are strange herbs, bats' blood, toads' parts, soot gathered from unholy places and human bones. Some spells also call for human fat and more unthinkable things.

With these charms and potions a witch could presumably cause grain to rot and bread to turn black; she could keep seed from sprouting and make storm clouds roll. On the other hand, for a sufficient price a witch or sorcerer might put out a fire, stop a storm or an epidemic of illness, or—as in the case of the Pied Piper—rid a town of a plague brought by rats.

Witch Hunts

Some of the methods for finding witches seem cruel today. It was thought that a witch would not sink if she were thrown into the water. So women suspected of being witches were thrown into ponds with their hands tied. If they floated, they were condemned as witches. If they sank, they were considered innocent—but of course they often drowned.

A witch was supposed to have a mark of her pact with the devil somewhere on her body. (When a Witches' Sabbath was at hand a tingling of this mark was supposed to alert her.) At this spot she could feel no pain. So one test was to prick a woman all over with pins or needles. If she did not seem to suffer when some one spot was pricked, that "proved" she was a witch. It did not pay to try to be brave in this test!

From about the year 1000 to less than 200 years ago, it appears that millions of women were executed as witches, mostly by being burned alive. Surely the number must have been very large. For once accused, perhaps by a jealous neighbor or, in the case of the Salem, Massachusetts, witch trials of colonial times, by hysterical children, it was very difficult to prove one's innocence. And some women truly believed in their own evil powers!

Protection and Exorcism

Because witches were believed to be so common, people felt a need to have protection against their powers. Many charms were sold and worn to guard their owners against the power of witches. The sprinkling of holy water, the use of rosaries and other talismans (to counteract those of the witches) were developed for the purpose of repulsing devils or those witches who were in the power of demons. Putting your hand over your mouth when you yawn is a custom that was started to keep evil spirits from popping into the inviting opening. Above all, the sign or sight of the Christian cross was supposed to render any witch or devil powerless.

Many churches still have special services of exorcism which use some holy talismans and prayers to drive out evil spirits that may be possessing or haunting a person or place.

Some farmers still decorate their barns with designs called hex marks (hexe is the German word for witch) against supernatural powers that might, for example, dry up or sour the milk of the farmers' cows.

Witch Doctors and Medicine Men

Witchcraft is still taken very seriously in lands as far apart as tropical Africa, Australia, Southeast Asia and Melanesia (a group of Pacific islands). And those who practice it properly are often highly respected, even feared for their supernatural powers.

by trembling, rapid breathing, or some other departure from usual behavior?

Other apparent powers of people alleged to be modern witches are truly mysterious and awesome. People have fallen ill and died when witches and shamans put a curse on them or stuck pins into a wax image of them. Some "witches" have demonstrated amazing power over the minds of those who believe in them. And sometimes, it is claimed, they can exert their power even over those who scoff at them.

In recent years there has been a resurgence of interest on the part of some young people in the United States in witchcraft and demon-worship. The willingness of some of these young people to follow leaders blindly has led to some extremely brutal deeds and to even more ruined lives. The attraction of this kind of witchcraft is really a mystery—and an eerie one at that.

On some islands of the South Pacific any boat bringing visitors is met by a witch doctor who removes any evil spirits that may be aboard. In many African communities most illnesses are treated by witch doctors or medicine men with medicinal herbs or other charms given added strength by the faith of the patients.

If a robbery or other crime occurs, a witch doctor can often discover the guilty person by the use of his bag of magic charms—and his knowledge of his people and how they respond.

Though a witch doctor relies somewhat for his effectiveness on charms such as bones, skin or whole skeletons of small animals, snakes and the like, his true power seems to rest in large part on applied psychology.

Let us say that a theft has occurred in a small African village. The people concerned are gathered together, and the witch doctor is called. He lays out his charms, reciting incantations as he does so. All present are confident that he will indeed uncover the identity of the culprit. Is it not to be expected that the guilty one will betray his fear of discovery and punishment

Sorcery and Spells

Sorcerers are masters of spells and *sortes* (the singular is a *sors*). Many of the most famous sorcerers were involved with forecasting the future. Originally a *sors* was a slip of paper. In sorcery, people used to write a whole set of quotations from a favorite author on a batch of slips, put them all into an urn and have someone draw out one at random. Its content was supposed to suggest the future.

A variation that was popular in the Middle Ages and is still in use is to open a Bible at a chance page, then, with eyes closed, place a fingertip on some verse. That verse should provide some hint as to the future.

A few years ago the inefficiency of the manager in a small office was causing distress to other workers. When three of the workers met one day to discuss the problem, one blindly put a finger on a Bible verse. It read: "How are the mighty fallen in the midst of the battle." Shortly thereafter the manager was replaced.

In other cultures entrails of a freshly killed chicken were consulted by sorcerers, who believed that the color and condition of the parts provided clues to the future. Or letters of the alphabet were written on grains of corn or wheat and a cock was allowed to eat the scattered kernels. The sorcerer noted the order in which the "letters" were eaten to get the mystic message.

Sorcerers, or diviners, had almost limitless methods. Some carried small sacks containing magic talismans—bones, sticks, stones. When these were tossed out on a cloth and their arrangement was studied, it provided information to the knowledgeable.

Others marked knuckle bones with letters or dots. These developed into sets of dice whose patterns could be understood by those blessed with the power of sorcery. The Chinese used sets of special sticks with mystic markings.

Grain or sand were sometimes tossed out onto a cloth and the patterns studied. Peas were thrown into a fire, and if they burned quickly the forecast was considered good. Or straws were burned, and the twisting shapes they made as they crumbled gave information. Rings formed by dropping a bit of oil onto a pot of water also provided messages which could be read.

Special sets of cards—tarot or others—were sometimes laid out in a wide variety of patterns. Or a key suspended from a thread dangling from a finger provided the answers to questions. (See "Fortunetelling.")

Ancient Greece had an oracle—a priestess who was supposed to have the gift of prophecy—so famous that people came from far and wide to consult her. (If we assume that all oracles worked by sorcery, this must have been a sorceress.) She lived in a temple on the side of a mountain at Delphi and was known as the Delphic Oracle.

She sat in a darkened room and could be consulted only by a priest of the temple. Some people think that underground gases came up through a hole in the temple floor where she sat and put the oracle into a kind of trance.

The forecasts she uttered were often very difficult to understand. Before one famous battle she sent word to the king who consulted her, Croesus of Lydia, that in the battle a great kingdom would be destroyed. No matter who won and who lost, that forecast was likely to come true. As it turned out, it was Croesus' own kingdom that was destroyed.

Spells and Philters

A fearsome talisman called the Hand of Glory was prepared by some sorcerers for robbers to use as they went about their work. Its preparation started with cutting off the hand of a hanged criminal. This had to be wrapped in cloth, placed in a pot with various herbs and minerals and left for two weeks, after which it was to be dried in the sun.

Sight of the Hand of Glory was supposed to temporarily paralyze anyone to whom it was shown—*unless* that person had had the forethought to rub his doorstep with a potion made of "the gall of a black cat, the fat of a white hen, and the blood of a screech-owl."

For double effectiveness, the Hand of Glory could be used as a holder for a special candle compounded of human fat, horse dung and various other ingredients.

Sorcerers made frequent use of a Magic Candle—always made of human fat—which was particularly helpful in discovering treasure hidden underground, since it sparkled and sputtered noisily as one approached the buried treasure.

Old books of instructions for sorcerers gave long invocations to be repeated if one wished to become invisible. But it was also said to be possible to attain invisibility by carrying a frog—or the heart of a bat—under one's right armpit.

Love Charms

To win the love of someone who is unresponsive, according to experts of long ago, it is necessary only to grind to powder "the heart of a dove, the liver of a sparrow, the womb of a swallow, the kidney of a hare" and to mix with these an equal part of one's own blood. Once the object of one's affections has downed an ounce or two of this special and rare potion, he or she will be in your power.

If you can wait until Midsummer's Eve, when in some lands ferns magically burst into bloom, plucking one of those blossoms at midnight, in the company of your loved one, will almost guarantee you success. Or try a mixture of powdered root of the pasque-flower or dane-blood, gathered on this evening, with ground orange, ambergris (from whales) and a bit of paper on which one has written the word *sheva* (which stands for a neutral vowel sound!).

Other charms—for inducing love as well as for other magical purposes—often involved the use of pentacles. A pentacle is a mathematical design with magical properties. Technically it should be a five-pointed design, since *penta* is the Greek and Latin root for "five." Actually many of the diagrams involve double triangles which form a six-pointed star, and some are constructed of interwoven crosses and squares. In addition, magical words and often Hebrew characters appear in the designs.

Death spells were most commonly cast with the help of a small waxen image into which pins or needles were stuck. Alternately, the image could be struck with a blunt instrument or melted down.

The power of sorcerers and their spells was feared sufficiently so that extreme tortures and often death by burning were meted out to those found guilty of practicing these arts in many European lands.

Just how much power they actually had is still a mystery today.

Alchemy

In a dim workroom long-robed men leaned anxiously over an arrangement of jugs and jars. One jar stood over a fire that crackled on a brick hearth. From this jar, steam and liquid bubbled and smoked, dripping slowly through long spouts into the waiting jugs.

The men muttered under their breath as they watched. To a listener it seemed that they were murmuring magical incantations. For these were alchemists. They were trying to transform lead into gold.

It was an ancient dream of man that other metals could somehow be turned to precious gold. A part of the idea behind the dream may have come from the teachings of Aristotle, a truly great scientific thinker of ancient Greece.

Aristotle believed the then current theory that all matter is made of four elements—fire, air, water and earth. All things were thought to be hot, cold, liquid or dry in various proportions and combinations. He also believed that all things move toward perfection. Gold was the perfect metal. Nature had made gold slowly from other metals, deep underground. Man, then, should be able to duplicate nature's process in a laboratory.

To make precious gold was the principal goal of alchemists. But they worked and worked, year after year, without success. Young boys came into laboratories as apprentices and grew old without seeing any progress in deriving the valuable mineral from inexpensive lead.

Alchemists did learn a good deal about how fire and acids and other substances can cause metals to change their form. Some of them also did good work at transforming the juices of plants into useful medicines. Their experiments, as the word *alchemy* (al-chemy) suggests, formed the basis of the modern science of chemistry.

Alchemists worked on for hundreds of years, in many lands from China to Egypt, Spain and northern Europe. Monks and emperors, scientists and pharmacists took part in the search for the magical substance they called the philosopher's stone or the philosopher's egg. They considered it the symbol of creation, the perfect element, containing in one the four basic elements of matter—fire, air, water and earth. They believed that it could convert all other metals into pure gold.

As they worked, some were content to turn out metals for jewelry making that imitated gold and silver. Others insisted that they had really succeeded in their quest. They put on elaborate shows in which they claimed to produce real gold. They relied on fakery, magic, even necromancy—the calling up of spirits. From these fakers, alchemy got a bad reputation. But they convinced some people of their success, stirring up greed in many hearts. Some alchemists, it is said, lived in fear of being robbed or murdered in their beds for their gold.

Modern chemists have learned a great deal about making new substances from old ones. The old alchemists would be astounded at some of the wonders of chemistry today—such as spinning fibers of silken softness from coal. But the mystery of the philosopher's stone that could turn lead into gold is still unsolved.

Fortunetelling

The mysterious work done in laboratories in olden days was then considered sorcery. Some of it has since developed into science. Other work once done by sorcerers in divination—the divining of the future—has in modern times been watered down to fortunetelling. Some people take this seriously, but many more enjoy it simply as a parlor trick.

In a corner of all but the most skeptical minds, though, a sense of wonder lingers. Hints as to future probabilities, and as to our own innermost feelings, talents and characteristics, are appealing to most of us. They can be found by following some of many paths discussed below.

Astrology—the Path of Stars and Planets

The "science" of reading character and fate in the pattern of planets and stars as they appeared at one's birth is a very old one. From its earliest appearance in history, perhaps as early as 3000 B.C. in Babylonia, until about 400 years ago, it was closely associated with astronomy—the scientific study of the universe.

The drawing of horoscopes based on the positions of the constellations and planets in the zodiac goes back to ancient Greece. The twelve signs of the zodiac are figures the ancients pictured in the sky. These were said to appear and disappear during the year within the band of sky marked by the sun, moon and planets.

The basic idea behind astrology is that the alignment of heavenly bodies around the earth at the time of one's birth—or conception—has a profound influence on one's nature.

At the time when astrological principles were laid down, the whole spectrum of electromagnetic waves had not been dreamed of. We now know that they influence our lives in many important ways. It seems wholly possible that there may be another as yet unidentified form of universal energy of equal importance that could explain many psychic phenomena.

Meanwhile, the reason why there should be a relationship between the angle at which rays from various heavenly bodies fell upon your birthplace at the hour of your birth, and your nature and response to life's challenges, remains a mystery.

So much "parlor trick" fortunetelling is done daily in newspapers and other publications in the name of astrology that it is easy to scoff at it. Interestingly, many people who have a deep interest in psychic phenomena are contemptuous of astrology and of those who believe in it.

Some astrologers who point backward to very specific and accurate forecasts they claim to have made are very vague when it comes to looking forward and putting themselves on record as to what is going to happen.

It is wise to have modest hopes as to what you will gain from having a horoscope cast or buying a booklet giving information about your—or someone else's—astrological "sign."

"Sun signs," says one well-known astrologer, "are far ahead of any other known quick, reliable method of analyzing people and learning to understand human nature. An individual's sun sign will be about 80 percent accurate."

A reasonably complete astrological reading for any individual takes hours to prepare and requires exact information as to the hour and place of birth. Even then chances are it will not give you an accurate timetable for your life, past or future. But as to general personality and character traits, whether a reading is scientific or not, it does seem to have much better than random accuracy.

Check these very scant hints about people born under each of the twelve signs of the zodiac against your friends. Is the one that fits his or her birth date 80 percent accurate? Is it *more* accurate, taken as a whole, than any of the other eleven? (If the birth date falls near the beginning or end of a sign, the adjoining one may also apply and should also be read.)

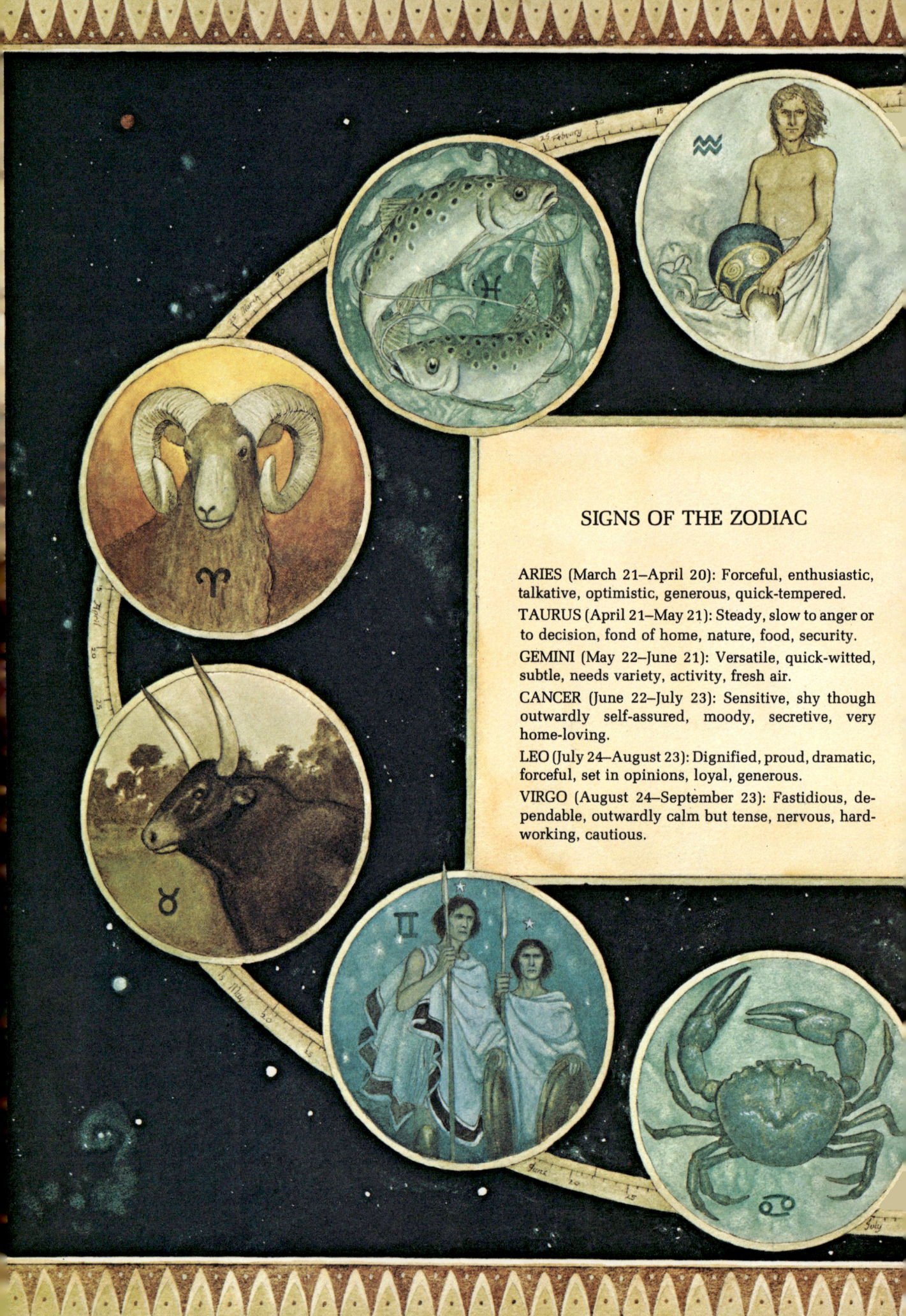

SIGNS OF THE ZODIAC

ARIES (March 21–April 20): Forceful, enthusiastic, talkative, optimistic, generous, quick-tempered.

TAURUS (April 21–May 21): Steady, slow to anger or to decision, fond of home, nature, food, security.

GEMINI (May 22–June 21): Versatile, quick-witted, subtle, needs variety, activity, fresh air.

CANCER (June 22–July 23): Sensitive, shy though outwardly self-assured, moody, secretive, very home-loving.

LEO (July 24–August 23): Dignified, proud, dramatic, forceful, set in opinions, loyal, generous.

VIRGO (August 24–September 23): Fastidious, dependable, outwardly calm but tense, nervous, hardworking, cautious.

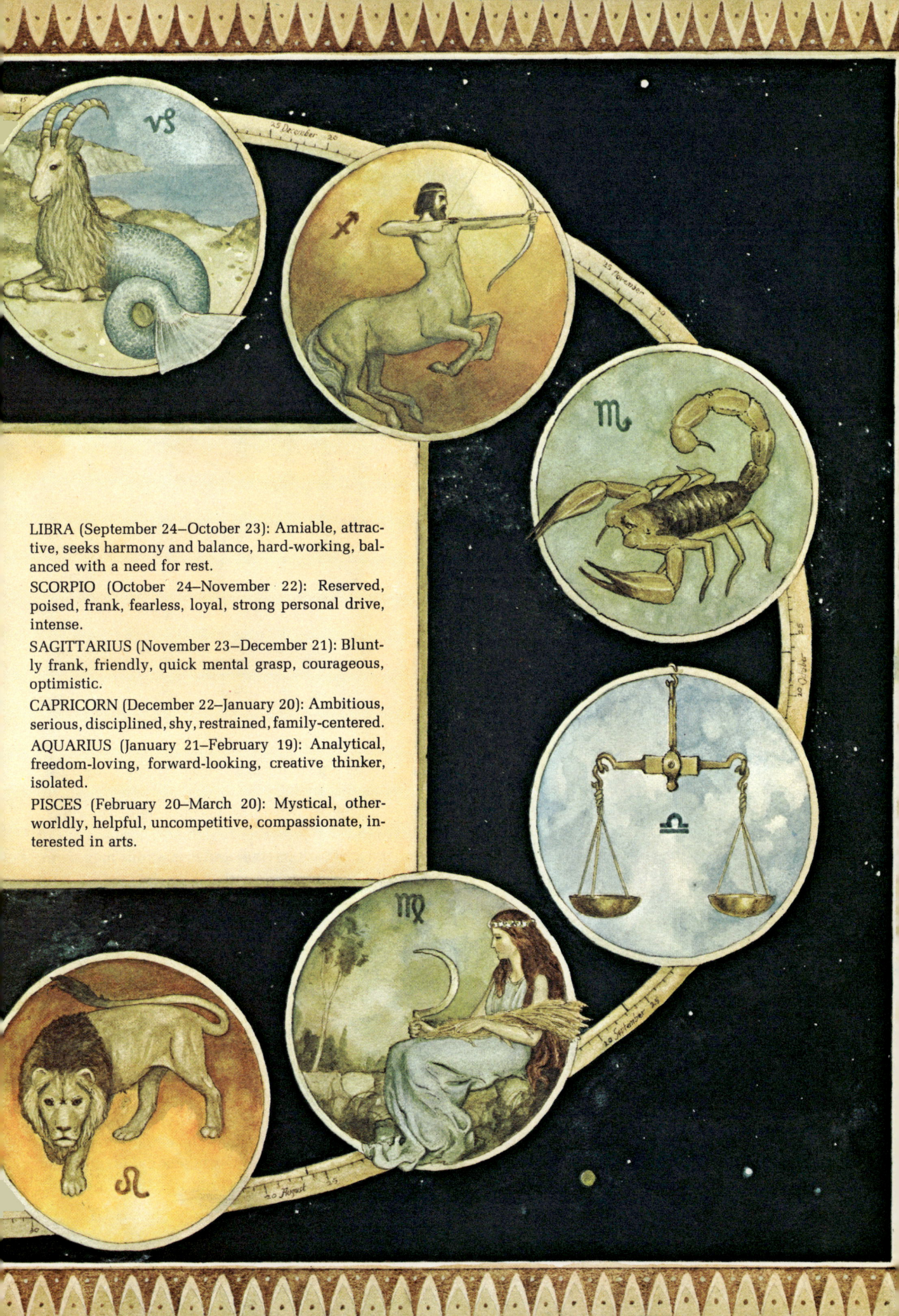

LIBRA (September 24–October 23): Amiable, attractive, seeks harmony and balance, hard-working, balanced with a need for rest.

SCORPIO (October 24–November 22): Reserved, poised, frank, fearless, loyal, strong personal drive, intense.

SAGITTARIUS (November 23–December 21): Bluntly frank, friendly, quick mental grasp, courageous, optimistic.

CAPRICORN (December 22–January 20): Ambitious, serious, disciplined, shy, restrained, family-centered.

AQUARIUS (January 21–February 19): Analytical, freedom-loving, forward-looking, creative thinker, isolated.

PISCES (February 20–March 20): Mystical, otherworldly, helpful, uncompetitive, compassionate, interested in arts.

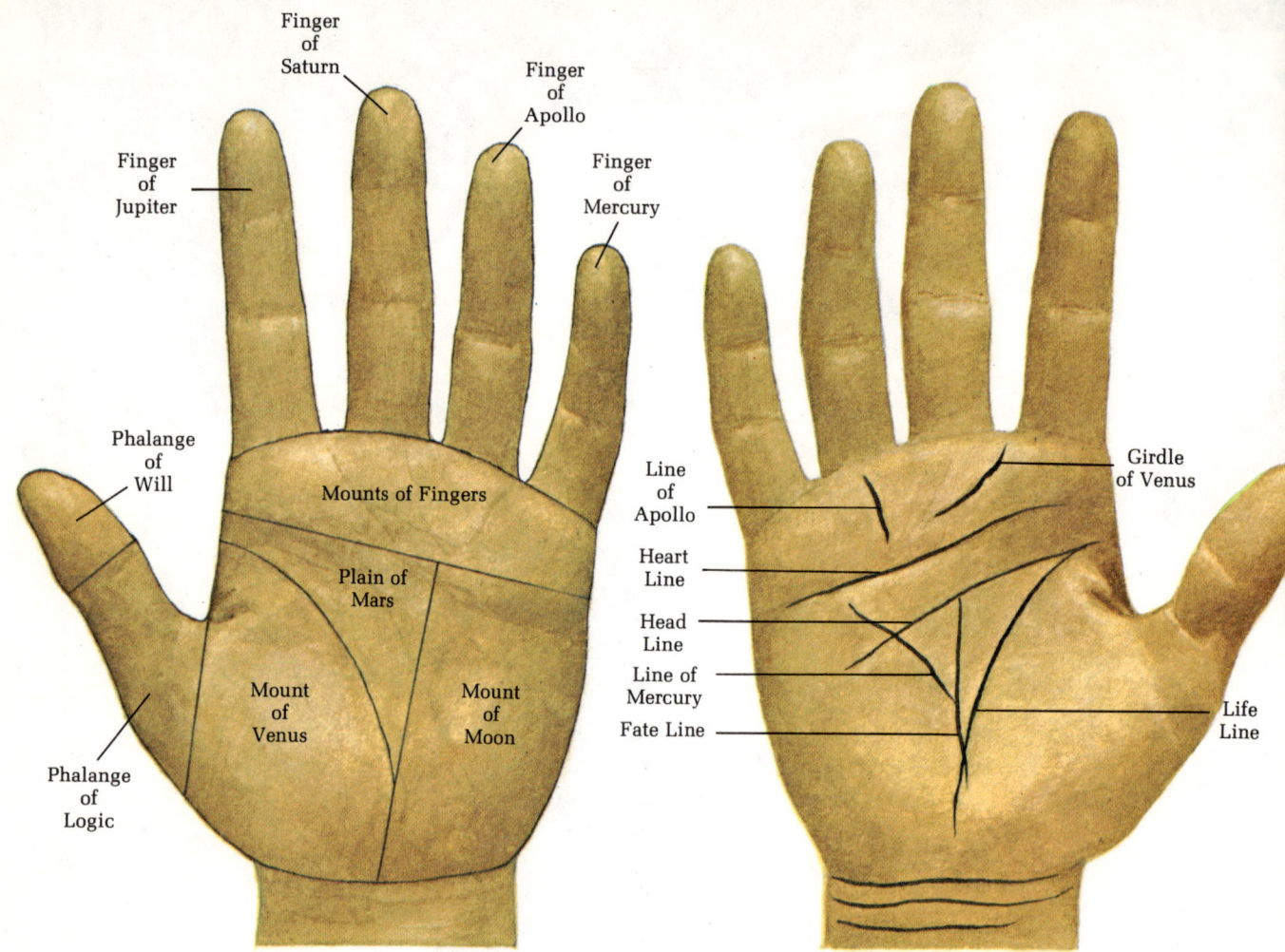

Palmistry

Five thousand years ago in China, people studied the lines and folds of hands for clues to character and to some extent to fate. This system was also popular in ancient Greece, Rome and Egypt, in India (from which it was carried to many lands by wandering gypsies) and among Hebrew and Arab peoples.

The eleventh edition of the Encyclopaedia Britannica, published in 1910, describes the anatomical purposes of the various folds and swellings of the palm—to permit bending, prevent slipping of the grip and so on. It concludes its discussion with this comment: "That these purely mechanical arrangements have any psychic, occult or predictive meaning is a fantastic imagination, which seems to have a peculiar attraction for certain types of mind, and as there can be no fundamental hypothesis of correlation, its discussion does not lie within the province of reason."

The type of mind attracted to this study, however, has included many highly trained in scientific fields, including psychiatrists. They have found that, however fanciful the assignment of traits to various lines and formations may seem, there is actually a rather high correlation with objective observations.

It is possible, for example, for a person moderately skilled in hand-reading to give quick, superficial but pointed readings to a group of people he does not know who, however, know one another rather well. And they will (or have in specific instances) agree that each reading bore a much more than chance relation to the person as friends knew him or her.

As in the case of astrology, many writers, in an attempt to give their work popular appeal, assign arbitrary meanings to certain markings. Claiming that "a domestic scandal is indicated by an island on the Line of Marriage" is an example of this, a kind of interpretation that lessens the credibility of the whole system.

Only a few very general principles can be given in the space available here. But it is very interesting to do careful palm reading, horoscope and handwriting analysis of the same person. However skeptical an observer may be, he is almost certain to be impressed by the high degree of agreement among the three character readings.

Hand shape:
Broad, short palms: hard-driving, extroverted.
Narrow, long palms: thoughtful, introverted.
Small palms: big plans, clever, easily bored.
Large palms: patient with detail.
Square palm and fingers: practical, conventional, orderly.
Flared or spatula-shaped palm and fingers: original thinker, creative.
Tapering or conic palm and fingers: appreciative, love of beauty.
Hard, knotted or philosophic palm and fingers: curious, observant, slow to decide.
Long, fragile, psychic hand: visionary, intuitive, lacking in energy and sense of order.

Lines on palms:
Main lines deep, clearly marked: strong sense of purpose, deep feelings.
Main lines fine, faltering: impressionable, nervous.
Many lines deeply marked: deep feelings, emotional.
Many fine lines: inner conflict, nerves.
Few, simple lines: concentration, few strong interests.

Emphasis in hand:
Leaning toward forefinger: ambitious, dominant, practical.
Leaning toward ring finger: artistic, less worldly.
Leaning toward little finger: highly intuitive.
Dominated by second finger: sober, pensive, moody.
Wrist third of palm dominant: earthy, physical, impulsive.
Center third of palm dominant: practical drive.
Upper third of palm dominant: intellectual, original.

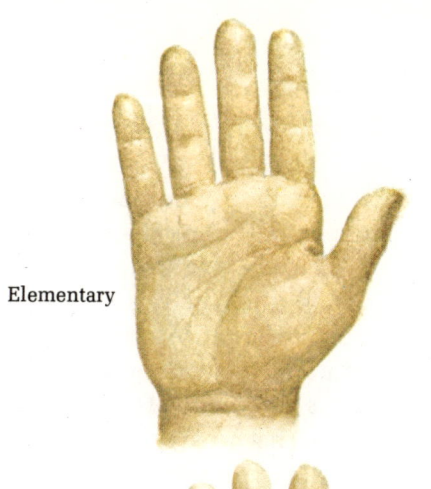
Elementary

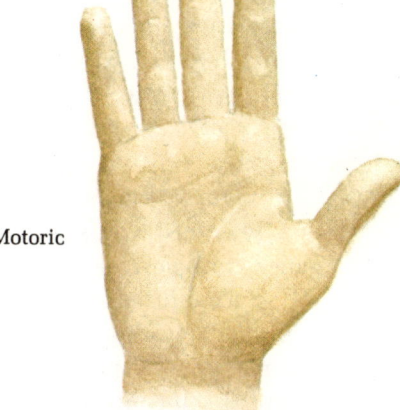
Motoric

THE FOUR BASIC
HAND TYPES OF CARUS

Sensitive

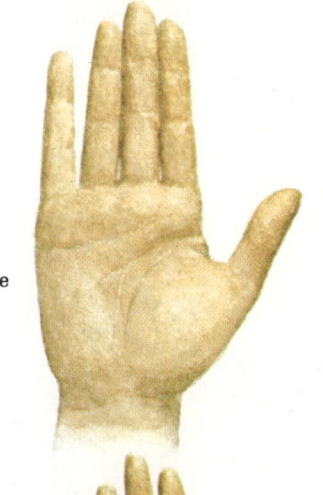
Psychic

Handwriting Analysis —Graphology

Even those skeptics who scorn most techniques for reading characters or fates are willing to concede that there may be some merit to handwriting analysis. Some personnel departments in large firms check handwriting samples before hiring employees. Some police departments also use it. Many technical and scientific studies have been done in the field.

Still there are many mysteries connected with it. It is easy enough to say that handwriting whose lines slope upward reflects an optimistic approach to life, while lines that run downhill seem pessimistic or gloomy. This may reflect just a change in mood rather than a basic character trait.

Similarly, it is easy to claim that extremely widely spaced words and lines suggest extravagance, while extremely tight overlapping lines reflect a confused and muddled person. In general small writing suggests high intelligence. But many more specific characteristics such as shyness, self-control, ambition, judgment, concentration and initiative can also be judged. So can stubbornness, argumentativeness, deceitfulness, overaggressiveness and vulgarity. Recognizing some of these takes a good deal of study, and some of the clues seem mysterious to a casual observer.

Phrenology—Reading the Head

If folds and creases, pads of muscle and texture of skin in the hands can be indications of character, it would seem logical that the shape of the head might be too. In the mid-nineteenth century, for a time "reading" the bumps and hollows of the skull and the features of the face enjoyed quite a vogue.

Surely none of us can deny that we form our first opinions of people we meet, in part at least, on the basis of appearance. We might be inclined to go along in general with "principles" such as these:

EYES: *wide-open:* eager, naïve; *partly open:* shrewd, keen; *very narrowed:* tricky, suspicious; *wide apart:* trusting, generous; *close set:* suspicious, calculating. *Blue*—optimistic, energetic, reasonable; *gray or pale blue*—businesslike, successful, cool or cold; *green*—energetic, talented, temperamental; *hazel*—gentle, affectionate; *brown*—emotional, artistic, intense.

MOUTH: *small*—small-minded, prim, selfish; *large*—generous, tolerant; *turned up*—cheerful; *turned down*—gloomy; *straight*—balanced; *thick lips*—sensual; *thin lips*—cold, determined; *short upper lip*—vain; *long upper lip*—ambitious, persistent; *lower lip and chin short*—weak; *lower lip and chin long*—determined.

Most of us, however, can think of friends who represent exceptions to these so-called rules.

As for the system considered scientific in the mid-1800s, its discussions of such traits as "alimentiveness" and "eventuality" (love of life, appetite and memory) contribute as much to an air of mystery as to understanding.

To give some inkling of the technique employed, here is a sample: Draw a line from the outer point of the eye to the top of the ear. "Destructiveness" extends upward from this point about a half an inch. "Secretiveness" is three-quarters of an inch above the middle of the top of the ears, rounding out the head if it is large. Extend the line from the top of the ears backward an inch and a half and you are on "combativeness." To find "parental love," extend the line to the middle of the back of the head. Three-fourths of an inch above parental love is "inhabitiveness"—or "love of home"—which, in the negative, may cause a small depression

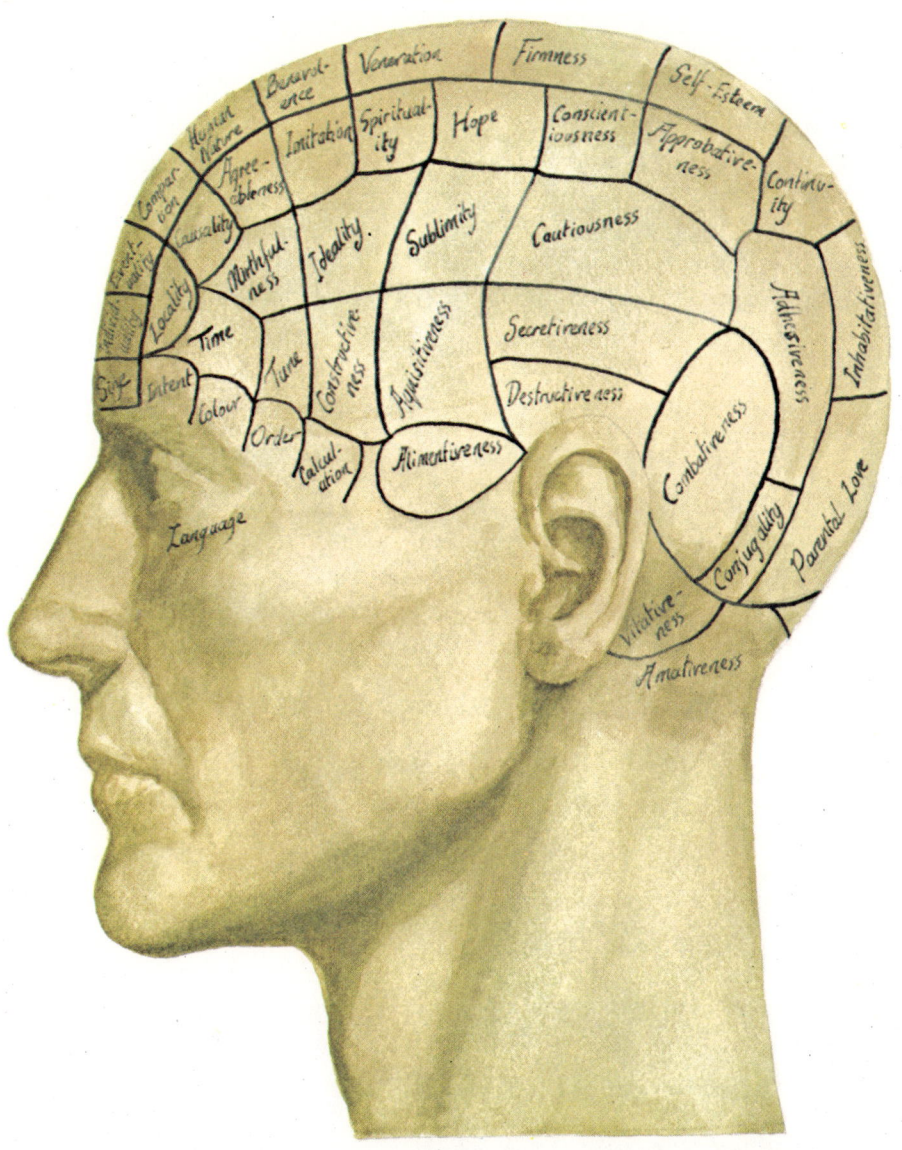

rather than a bump. An inch to each side is "friendship." "Amativeness"—sexual love—lies an inch and a half back from the midpoint of the ear, and so on.

One more example: Draw another line, starting from the opening of the ear, straight up to the mid-top of the head. You have found "firmness." An inch and a half back of firmness is "self-esteem," and about an inch to either side of self-esteem lies "approbativeness." Self-esteem is described in terms of self-respect, nobleness and dignity. Approbativeness is equated with love of popularity, vanity and regard for appearances. And one practitioner of phrenology said firmly: "In nineteen females out of every twenty, approbativeness will be found considerably larger than self-esteem."

Ability to communicate through language is located behind the eyes, we are told, causing them to bulge and the lids to appear puffed and swollen. People with deeply set eyes presumably have difficulty in expressing themselves.

The entire human skull has been analyzed by phrenologists—and often compared with skulls of tigers, crows and other animals. In view of the popularity of the occult and related systems of "knowledge," it is perhaps the near disappearance of phrenology that is the real mystery.

Crystal Balls—Tools of Fortune

"What do you see in your crystal ball?" we may ask a friend, partly in jest, when we are trying to make some plan for the future. For crystal gazing was one of the earliest forms of forecasting the future.

Actually a mirror was often used by the ancients—a mirror of polished brass or the smooth surface of a pool of water. The magic mirror might be held up to the moon for extra power before the reading. Sometimes precious stones were substituted for the mirror, since for certain persons gazing intently at them could disclose the future or the answer to questions.

It is hard to discover just where and when spheres or egg-shaped balls of clear rock crystal or glass were first used. Certainly they have long been in use in Hindu and some Buddhist circles. Crystal is thought to have a special magnetism for spiritual forces. The power to "read" a crystal seems to be related to clairvoyance.

A crystal ball needs to be handled with care and well guarded, especially when in use, from light, reflections and sound. This is why readings are often held in dimly lighted, heavily draped rooms where the seer tenderly lifts a covering of dark velvet from the globe and then makes a few passes with the hand close to the surface to increase its magnetism.

The Crystal Skull

Perhaps the most perfect example of the mysterious powers of crystal is the crystal skull found in a Mayan ruin in Central America in 1927.

The skull is the size and shape of a human skull. It is hewn out of a solid piece of transparent crystal. The smoothness of its finish suggests that no metal tool ever touched it. One authority has estimated that it must have taken 300 years of constant human labor to grind it out of a block of rock.

The jaw has been separated from the skull. When balanced correctly, the skull nods, the jaw opening and closing. This feature has made some of the numerous scientists who have studied it wonder if it was used as an oracle,

with its moving jaw and nodding head signifying Yes and No.

It is also possible that it was used in the same way as plain crystal balls, into which one gazes hoping for a scene to appear. But this crystal skull has powers far beyond those of most gazing spheres.

For one thing, no one has been able to assign it to a clear place in the archaeology of the Mayans—or of any other people in any land or time. One enthusiast claims it is an 11,000-year-old relic of lost Atlantis. (See page 130.)

In addition the crystal affects all five senses. It changes color and transparency, and an eighteen-inch halo has been observed surrounding it. It rings with faint high-pitched sounds like silver bells. Periodically it emits an unmistakable odor. It makes observers thirsty. And when the fingers of sensitive viewers touch the skull they experience distinct feelings of heat and cold as well as vibrations suggesting an energy source.

The mysterious properties of the crystal skull have not been scientifically explained.

A Swinging Answer

Cleidomancy was the name given in olden times to a method of divination in which a thread was attached to the nail of a virgin's ring finger, and a key was hung from the other end of the thread. A question could then be asked, and if the answer was affirmative, the key would revolve at the end of the thread.

"Oh, we did that same sort of thing," says a woman reared in Central Europe, "with any small object hanging from a ribbon or light chain. It was called the magic eye."

A variation with requirements less rigid than those for cleidomancy still works for many people today. A very small crystal ball makes the ideal weight, but if one is not available any small symmetrical object with enough weight to hang firmly from its cord but light enough to move easily will be suitable.

Before embarking, it is important to hold the object in one's hands for a few moments, stroking it lightly, to magnetize it with the body's psychic energy. Then run through the "code" of responses several times, causing the object to swing in the appropriate pattern as you softly repeat the responses.

"Yes" is represented by a forward and back swing, "No" by a side-to-side swing; "I don't know" is indicated by a clockwise circular motion, "I do not choose to answer" by a counter-clockwise circling.

When a quesion is asked, the operator should rest his or her elbows firmly on a table, with fingertips meeting lightly at the peak of the pyramid formed by the operator's hands. The chain or cord must be grasped lightly between right thumb and forefinger so that the "magic eye" hangs just free of the table. Wait until it hangs perfectly still. Then repeat the question several times softly—preferably with eyes closed for added concentration.

Soon, as psychic power flows from the fingertips into the chain or cord, you may feel a slight tingling in the thumb and fingertip. This indicates that the answer is being given. When you open your eyes you will find that the small object is indeed moving gently in one of the answer patterns—and very likely not the one you had in mind!

A man with a record of considerable success with this method reports that one evening, annoyed by a series of "I do not choose to answer" replies to a question he had asked, he flung his small crystal ball, chain and all, against the far wall of the room. As it struck, all the lights in the house went out. No, it was not a blown fuse. The reason is still a mystery.

Tarot Cards

The origin of today's playing—and fortunetelling—cards is shrouded in mystery. It can be traced back as far as fourteenth-century Germany, but beyond that everything becomes hazy. Some claim Egyptian or Jewish origins for the pictured cards.

The four suits of the tarot—cups, swords, coins and staffs—originally represented the four principal classes of the social world of the Middle Ages. The cup or chalice stood for the churchmen, the sword for the knights and soldiers, the coin for the merchants and the staff for the farm folk.

Early sets of tarot cards fell into two distinct types. One was similar to modern decks of cards. Each of the four suits had cards numbered from one to ten and a king, queen, knave or jack—and often a knight as well. This set was called the minor arcana, or mystery.

The major arcana consisted of twenty-two picture cards, each of which represented some phase in the journey of life. These cards were as follows:

1. *The Fool:* innocence or extravagance
2. *The Magician:* the beginning of learning
3. *The Priestess:* feminine influence and intuition
4. *The Empress:* motherhood and the creative force of nature
5. *The Emperor:* authority and masculine energy
6. *The High Priest:* wisdom and enlightenment
7. *The Lovers:* choice of a mate
8. *The Chariot of the Sun:* adjustment to laws of society, triumph
9. *Justice:* the voice of conscience, justice
10. *The Hermit:* mature self-examination, wisdom
11. *The Wheel of Fortune:* all the ups and downs of life, wealth
12. *Strength:* courage to take a risk, strength
13. *The Hanged Man:* mature values and aims, prudence
14. *Death:* destruction making way for the new
15. *Temperance:* mature balance between wishes and behavior
16. *The Devil:* dangers along the journey of life
17. *The Tower Struck by Lightning:* undeserved disaster
18. *The Star:* greater awareness and future possibilities
19. *The Moon:* intuition and faith
20. *The Sun:* reconciliation of opposites, science and light
21. *Judgment:* coming together of one's mortal and immortal selves
22. *The World:* psychic wholeness, travel

Both sets are still in use. Either can be laid out in a wide variety of arrangements for a fortunetelling. Modern decks of cards may also be used, with spades (the equivalent of swords) generally meaning unhappiness; hearts (cups), happiness; diamonds (staffs), news; clubs (coins), money. Power increases with the number—ten being much stronger than two. The face cards represent people of the sex and coloring pictured. Generally spades suggest evil persons.

Often, however, particular layouts give their own meanings to cards. One simple method involves having the subject shuffle a complete pack of cards and cut it with the left hand into three smaller packs. These he turns face up. The

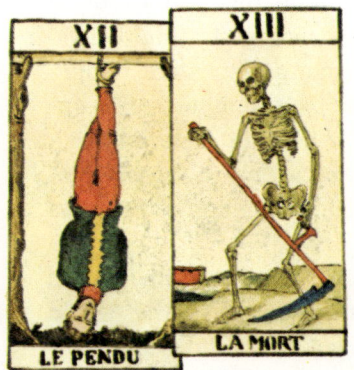

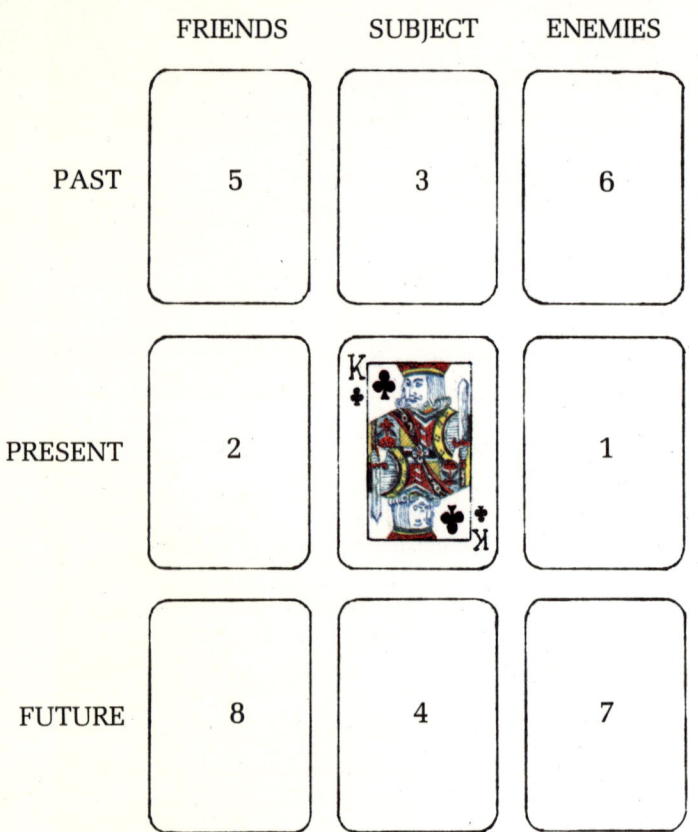

The king, queen or jack of a suit is selected to represent the subject and is placed in the center of the table. The sevens, eights, nines and tens of the four suits are then removed from the pack. These are shuffled, and eight of them are laid out to form a magic square around the subject. The cards should be laid out in the following order: right, left, above, below, upper left, upper right, lower right, lower left.

The upper row now represents the past, the center the present and the lower row the future. The left-hand row represents friends of the subject, the center row the subject himself, the right-hand row persons opposed to the subject. The cards and suits have the usual values.

The tarot and other card fortunetelling systems have at various periods acquired such power over people's minds that they came to be called "the devil's pasteboards." Various rulers even banned their use by law.

If the fortunes are accepted lightly, though, they can provide an amusing pastime occasionally spiced with rather remarkable touches of clairvoyance or telepathy.

three cards are read as they face the subject. Only the aces really have an "up and down." If the central symbol is upside down as it faces the subject, its meaning is reversed.

Thus, hearts stand for joy and often romance. The ace means pleasant news in this connection; if reversed, unpleasant news. Heart face cards represent pleasant, warm people. The number cards represent varying degrees of success, joy or affection. The nine of hearts is the wish card and means that the subject's dearest wish will be granted.

Diamonds suggest quarrels and difficulties. The ace of diamonds means pleasant anticipation when face up; reversed, frustrating delays. The face cards of diamonds represent people who cause difficulties, the number cards annoyances and delays of varying importance.

Clubs in a similar way suggest modest prosperity and good fortune; spades speak of illness or loss.

Nine, like three, is a number with mystic power. So it is not surprising that the Magic Nine is also a much used fortunetelling layout.

Tea Leaves, Coffee Grounds

Coffee grounds can be read if they are dumped onto a small plate or saucer. If a few bits of tea leaves remain in the bottom of a teacup, they can also be read. The subject should turn the cup around three times by the handle, swinging it slightly to distribute the grounds. A man should turn the cup in a clockwise direction, a woman counterclockwise.

The reader holds the cup with the handle toward her. Past events are then seen to the left, the present in the center, the future to the right.

In general, straight lines are fortunate, while wavy ones suggest difficulties or losses. Circles filled mean money; rings mean marriage. Squares suggest happiness, while odd angular figures indicate discord. Triangles mean success in love.

Most fortunetelling systems depend for any degree of success upon the psychic sensitivity of the "teller," since any objective reason why tea leaves, coffee grounds, cards or other devices should have special knowledge is mysterious indeed.

MYSTERIOUS DISAPPEARANCES

Any mysterious disappearance, whether of a favorite tool or toy, a man or child, a ship at sea or plane in mid-air, haunts the mind and grates on one's sense of security. Bizarre legends, some of them dating from ancient times, have told of individuals, groups of people and in some instances whole civilizations that have vanished, sometimes leaving behind tantalizing clues, other times without a trace. While some of these tales may be fanciful, there have been enough strange occurrences, such as ships found without crews and whole settlements that have vanished, enough evidence of civilizations and peoples lost to history, to start one wondering.

Ships Without Crews

The Seabird

It was on a bright Sunday morning in 1850 that the *Seabird* appeared off Newport, Rhode Island, sailing straight toward deadly reefs. As onlookers watched, horrified, from the beach, the ship miraculously scudded safely over the reefs and went aground on the beach, apparently unharmed.

That was rather strange, but stranger still was the fact that no sailors appeared. When men from the beach boarded the vessel, they found not a soul, dead or alive.

A pot of coffee bubbled on the stove in the galley. Instruments were in order, and the ship's log was up to date. In fact the last entry had been made only a few miles off Newport. But in the short time it took the ship to sail those few miles, captain and crew had vanished.

The ship carried a load of coffee and lumber from Central America, which was found and removed. Freed of its weight, the *Seabird* floated free at high tide during the night—and vanished as completely as its crew!

The Marie Celeste

Legends of the sea are filled with tales of ships that vanished without trace. But none of the tales of seamen and their ships is stranger than that of the *Marie Celeste*.

One December day a hundred years ago she was sighted near the Azores, heading westward. The crew of the brig that sighted her called out to the vessel. Receiving no answer and seeing no one on the decks, they went aboard.

They found things in fair condition, water-soaked but orderly. The cargo was safely

stowed, the quarters in order, the galley clean—but not a human being was aboard.

The final entry in the log book, November 25, 1872, gave no hint of trouble. But the sails were torn, the compass smashed, the hatches open and the helm loose. The safety boat was gone, and there were traces of a hasty departure by the crew. The captain's wife and child had been aboard with him, but there was no trace of them, nor any hint of violence.

For a century men have puzzled over the mystery. Could a waterspout have overwhelmed the ship, ripping some sails, bursting the hatches and terrifying the crew into abandoning ship? It seemed an unlikely action for a seasoned captain and crew.

Could sudden warm temperatures have caused the barrels of alcohol in the cargo to swell and threaten an explosion? The sailors who boarded and searched the ship found no trace of fumes or fire.

Or was the *Marie Celeste* sailing under some strange curse? Since on a later voyage the luckless ship was scuttled by captain and crew, the mystery will never be solved.

The Abandoned Blimp

It was during World War II that two fishermen on a beach near San Francisco saw a Navy blimp—a gas-filled balloon with a gondola below that carried a crew of two on submarine patrols—plunging down near them. They ran toward it and grabbed the tie lines as the gondola touched the beach. The wind dragged it from their grasp, but they noticed that the door of the gondola had swung open and no one was aboard.

The craft landed a few hours later nearby, but no record or trace of the crew could be found. Their life raft was still in place.

The blimp had not been out of sight for long. Two fishing boats had seen it dip low over the water a few hours before its first plunge to the beach. At that time the crew had radioed their base that they were checking on some oil slicks. The fishermen had seen the airship abruptly soar into the clouds and vanish there.

What happened to the two experienced Navy men up there in the clouds? Even the Navy admits that it is a complete mystery.

Into Thin Air

Draw a triangle over the Atlantic Ocean with Bermuda as its northeasterly point and a line along the Bahamas touching the coast of the United States as its southwesterly base. Somewhere above that stretch of ocean, during the last twenty years, more than twenty airplanes have vanished with passengers and crew without leaving a trace.

The first and perhaps most dramatic disappearance was that of a flight of Navy bombers on a training mission. Five planes were involved, each with a crew of two or three experienced men. They were in routine radio communication with the base until suddenly the flight commander radioed that he was not sure where they were. The crews of the five planes began talking anxiously among themselves.

"Looks like we are..." one was saying, when the voice broke off suddenly. That was the last word received from the planes.

A seaplane with a crew of thirteen took off from base on a rescue mission. Within five minutes it had vanished as completely as the rest.

Hundreds of planes and a score of ships, including a giant aircraft carrier, scoured the area. They found not a trace of oil slick or debris.

That was in 1945. In 1948 and again in 1949, four-motor British airliners bound from Bermuda to Jamaica vanished the same way and in clear skies.

And down through the years there have been other planes, private as well as commerical or military, that have flown into that triangle—to disappear into thin air.

Lost Settlements

Lost Roanoke

In 1587 the first English child born in the New World arrived at the Roanoke Island settlement off the coast of North Carolina. She was named Virginia Dare. Her birth seemed a happy omen for the little community of 121 pioneers, founded by Sir Walter Raleigh.

While Virginia was still a baby, a group from the settlement sailed back to England for supplies, and when they returned in 1590 or 1591, the village and all its people had vanished with hardly a trace.

The only clue was the word "Croatan" scrawled on the bark of a tree. This was the name of a nearby island—which has itself since vanished with the shifting of sands. At that time it was home to a tribe of Indians.

Was the village of Roanoke weakened by starvation and sickness, as happened to many other settlements? Did the survivors join the nearby Indians who were better equipped to support themselves? Are today's so-called Croatan Indians of North Carolina really, as they claim, descendants of both groups of sixteenth-century islanders, Indians and English? If so, where were they in 1590 when the English ship returned with fresh supplies?

The fate of the Lost Colony of Roanoke is still a mystery, like the tales of Viking colonies of 500 years earlier said to have been established far to the north and even deep inland.

Empty Eskimo Huts

In November 1930 a trapper on the Canadian tundra decided to visit a friendly Eskimo village and stumbled unaware onto a mystery.

The village was there, with kayaks drawn up on the beach and caribou-skin flaps still in place at the doorways of the huts. But no one answered his calls.

Curious, the trapper lifted one of the door flaps. No one was inside. He found dry and crusted food in the bottom of a pot over a burned-out fire. A bone needle still marked the partially completed mending of a child's sealskin jacket. But all the people had vanished—without rifles, dogs (they were found starved to death, tied to nearby trees) or boats.

Months of searching by the Canadian Mounted Police failed to turn up a single clue to the fate of the lost villagers.

ATLANTIS ACCORDING TO PLATO

Lost Civilizations

Atlantis

Back in ancient times an Egyptian priest told a tale to a Greek statesman. It was about a great island civilization that had been destroyed long before in an earthquake and had vanished under the sea. The statesman, named Solon, told the tale in turn to Plato, a philosopher and author. And Plato wrote about it in 335 B.C. Ever since, people have been speculating about the location of this mysterious land of Atlantis.

The original description placed Atlantis near the mythical Pillars of Hercules. This is a name associated with the rocky cliffs that border the entrance to the Straits of Gibraltar at the western end of the Mediterranean. The priest said the island had been "larger than Asia Minor and Libya" and that its civilization had flourished about 9000 B.C.

Both the size and the date seem highly improbable. The earliest civilizations on record date from about 4000 B.C., and the Mediterranean is hardly as big as Asia Minor. But it must be remembered that most people even today have rather vague ideas of distance and time beyond their own experience. This was even more true in the ancient world.

Down through the centuries many explanations have been offered and many sites have been suggested for Atlantis. The peninsula of Scandinavia and the Canary Islands in the Atlantic Ocean off Africa are among the plausible suggestions.

When America was discovered, Europeans were surprised to find that the Aztecs, Incas and Mayans had advanced civilizations. These peoples also had legends that described the sinking of their native lands and the travels of the displaced peoples to new homes. It pleased some Europeans to think that the original home of these American tribes might have been Atlantis.

Many others believe that early inhabitants of the Americas crossed the Bering Straits roughly 20,000 years ago when the Ice Age lowered the level of the seas and exposed a rocky stretch of land across the straits that formerly, and again in our time, separated the Asian and American continents. When the Ice Age ended, the melting ice raised the level of the seas, submerging the land link between Asia and North America under the rising waters. To many people this seems a more likely explanation for the legends of the "sinking motherlands" of Amerindians than the Atlantis story provides.

Descriptions of the ideal civilization of Atlantis grew more and more flowery through the

years. Some people visualized it as the Garden of Eden where all mankind had basked in a Golden Age. They felt that the Great Flood—which is found in mythologies the world over—was the catastrophe that drove mankind from Atlantis.

Others who remained skeptical viewed tales of Atlantis as just pleasant fiction. Then in 1967 ruins of a great submerged city began to be uncovered at Santorini, an island in the Aegean Sea. Santorini is today a small island, sloping down one side of an ancient volcanic crater. The other side of that great crater was blown away, it is thought today, in a huge explosion in about 1400 B.C. In that catastrophe, what had been a cone of rock several hundred feet high vanished, for the most part, beneath the sea. Ash was blown over an area of 80,000 square miles and piled up, close to the point of eruption, as much as 100 feet deep.

In 1400 B.C. Crete was the home of the Minoans, a sea-trading people. Through many centuries they had built up a brilliant civilization with rich art, a highly developed religion, comfortable homes with such "modern" conveniences as indoor plumbing, and with insurance companies that covered the risks of sea trade.

The Minoan civilization is known today largely through the ruins of its palaces and other fine buildings, for its era of greatness came to an abrupt end about 1400 B.C. in a catastrophe that wiped out many of its cities and left the buildings that did remain with fire-blackened walls.

The sudden collapse of the Minoans had long been a mystery. No one knew the cause of the catastrophe. Now with the uncovering of the remains of the lost civilization near Santorini, the Minoan tragedy would seem to fit neatly into a new version of the collapse of Atlantis.

The tidal waves and earthquakes that surely accompanied the explosion of the volcanic island now called Santorini would have demolished seaports, harbors and inland canals on Crete as well as on other Mediterranean islands. The whole area affected could well have been as large, roughly, as that Egyptian priest had described centuries ago.

Many people remember how the work of an archaeologist uncovered the ruins of Troy and so brought the story of the Trojan War out of legend and into history. They believe that excavations around Santorini are doing the same thing for the legend of Atlantis.

But some others still cling to their mystery. They recall the prophecy of the American psychic Edgar Cayce. In a trance he declared that the island of Atlantis would soon rise again from the depths of the Atlantic Ocean. So the clouds of mystery have not yet been completely swept away from Lost Atlantis.

Lemuria

According to some mystics even Atlantis was not the earliest of the civilizations on earth. The theosophists—people who feel that they have direct mystical knowledge of God and other truths that are hidden from most people—are among these. Long before Atlantis, they say, there was Lemuria.

We live, according to this theory, in the age of thought. Modern man must laboriously think out ways of doing things. The people of Atlantis did not have to bother with thinking. They had only to search their memories, for they stored away in memory all they needed to know. The people of Lemuria, living something like a million years before Atlantis' civilization, had instinctive knowledge of all they needed. As bees build their hives by instinct, so the Lemurians, in their land which the theosophists claim was located either somewhere south of Asia or in the Pacific off California, knew by instinct not only social principles but all about engineering and other practical arts.

The composition of the earth was also different in the time of these lost civilizations, according to this picture of the past. Air was thicker, water thinner. So in the days of Atlantis people had cars that could move smoothly on a cushion of the thicker air not far above the level of the ground.

How knowledge of these distant levels of life have come down to a few select human beings of the twentieth century is a mystery to the rest of us. And the source of the knowledge is a well-guarded secret.

One possible means of contact is through hypnosis. Certain individuals, under the spell of hypnosis, are said to recover memories of their lives in Atlantis or Lemuria. And one religious group claimed, within very recent years, that a small community of present-day Lemurians with the power to become invisible at will still lived deep in the mountain forests of California. Unfortunately the exact location of this community was not disclosed.

Vanished Peoples of the Past

Giants in the Earth?

"There were giants in the earth in those days," says Genesis, the first book of the Bible. And it goes on to explain them in these words: ". . . the sons of God came in unto the daughters of men, and they bore children to them; the same became mighty men. . . ."

Those mighty "giants in the earth" have long been a mystery to students of the Bible and others. Some people think that the "sons of God" referred to were actually visitors to earth from somewhere out in space, though none of the other planets in our solar system seems to be inhabited. And the closest other star is about twenty-five trillion miles from earth. That is too far to travel by any currently plausible means. But presumably the science and technology of the space visitors is much more advanced than ours. The people who believe in this visitors-from-another-world theory think that it was these strangers from outer space who started men on the long path of learning.

According to this theory, the "giants in the earth" were the offspring of the space visitors and their earthly brides. Perhaps as the space heritage thinned down during succeeding generations, the gigantic strain dwindled to the size range to which we are accustomed.

Some scattered traces of giants have been found. Skeletons of giants twelve feet tall and with double rows of teeth have been uncovered, according to unofficial reports, at more than one California site. Judging from objects found with the skeletons, it appears that these giants used stone axes, carved shells with strange symbols and ate not only seafood but the meat of small elephants of a kind thought to have vanished millions of years ago.

The burial case of another twelve-foot man—or one thought to be twelve feet tall, judging by the size of his coffin—was found in a rock tomb in Arizona, though the skeleton had long since turned to dust.

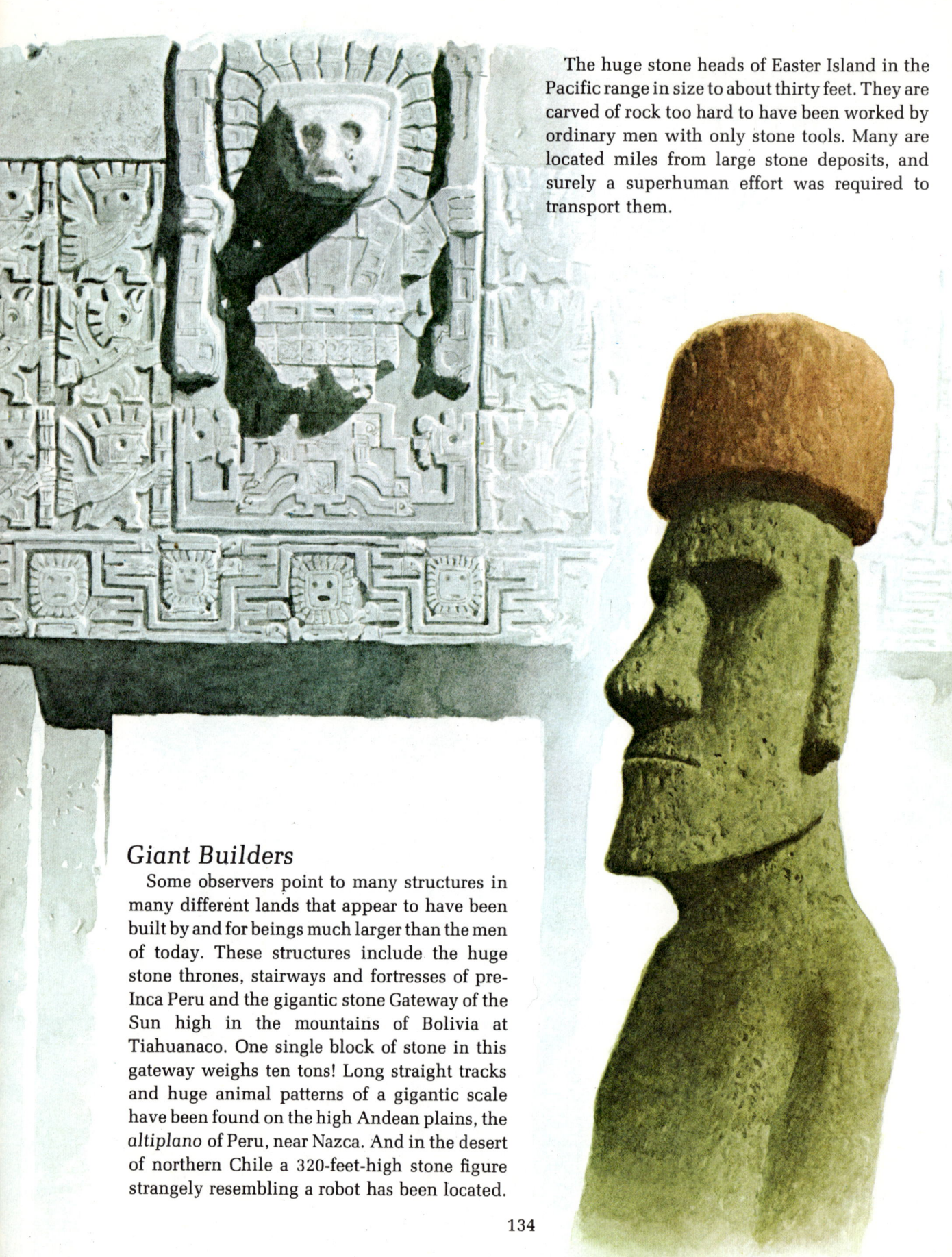

The huge stone heads of Easter Island in the Pacific range in size to about thirty feet. They are carved of rock too hard to have been worked by ordinary men with only stone tools. Many are located miles from large stone deposits, and surely a superhuman effort was required to transport them.

Giant Builders

Some observers point to many structures in many different lands that appear to have been built by and for beings much larger than the men of today. These structures include the huge stone thrones, stairways and fortresses of pre-Inca Peru and the gigantic stone Gateway of the Sun high in the mountains of Bolivia at Tiahuanaco. One single block of stone in this gateway weighs ten tons! Long straight tracks and huge animal patterns of a gigantic scale have been found on the high Andean plains, the *altiplano* of Peru, near Nazca. And in the desert of northern Chile a 320-feet-high stone figure strangely resembling a robot has been located.

In Costa Rica dozens of stone balls have been found, as much as seven feet in diameter. They are perfectly shaped spheres, smoothly worked. Some lie in forests where thick jungle growth has almost hidden them from view. Why they were put there and where and how and why they were made are complete mysteries.

There are also the immense prehistoric tomb markers, the dolmens and menhirs that dot the landscape from Ireland and England down through Western Europe and across the Mediterranean by way of Malta to North Africa. These tremendous blocks of rough stone towering upright or suspended between two uprights certainly suggest that the graves they mark might be those of giants in the earth.

Missing Links

Footprints left in mud that has hardened to rock through the ages and huge human teeth left in rock also suggest that tens of millions of years ago nature may have experimented with men much, much larger than even the twelve-footers whose skeletons have been found. Probably these huge human beings did not prove adaptable to their environment, and so they finally died out.

The rock walls of canyons near the Grand Canyon of the Colorado River show drawings clearly done by men. One shows a giant human fighting a mammoth—the elephantlike animal that appeared perhaps two million years ago and vanished between 35,000 and 25,000 years ago. Another pictures a dinosaur, the dreaded Tyrannosaurus Rex, which presumably died out seventy million or more years ago. This rock drawing raises another question: Did a few dinosaurs perhaps survive through long ages to the time of earliest man?

It appears that pre-humans lived on earth about two million years ago. These pre-humans were the ancestors of mankind and—following a different evolutionary path—of present-day apes. This common ancestor, or "missing link," is as yet unknown. But the Australopithecus, the closest thing yet found to the "missing link," was apparently about the same size as a short, stocky man of today. These remote beings walked upright and used simple tools. But they were far from the giants told of in the oldest legends handed down by people in lands all around the world, from ancient Greece to Japan.

So the case of the "giants in the earth" remains unsolved.

Lost Little People

Tales of "little people," often mischievous in their habits, are to be found in many lands. There are brownies, who creep into houses at night, drinking the saucers of milk left for the cats, nibbling the leftover food in kitchens, leaving trails of small muddy footprints across clean floors—but also doing helpful tasks in return for any favors done to them.

There are leprechauns in Ireland who reportedly sit at their doorways among tree roots, all but invisible in their leaf-green suits, forever tapping away at the mending of a single shoe—and guarding forever the pots of fairy gold they have hidden underground.

There are dwarfs who mined gold and jewels deep in rocky caves; pixies with their tricks; elves who made such excellent shoes by night for the poor cobbler in the old tale; fairies who stole human babies, leaving changelings—a different child—in their cribs. Are these all simply figments of imaginations that have everywhere delighted in the very small? Or do these little creatures have a basis in distant, dimly remembered fact?

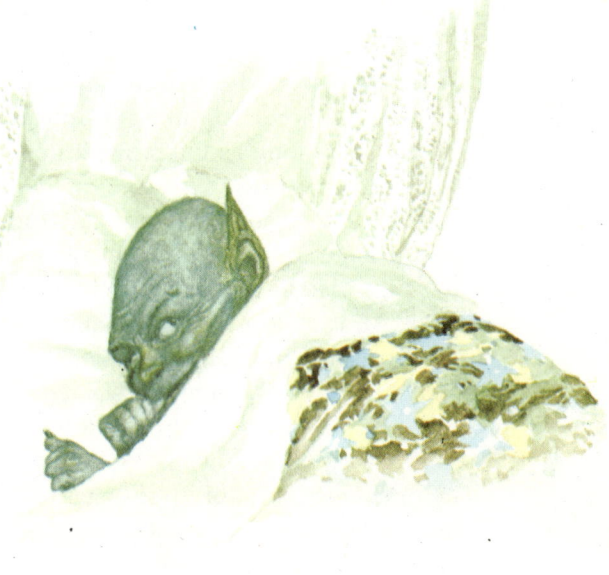

A Tiny Old Man

One story tells of a midget mummy found by prospectors in a Wyoming cave in 1932. These miners blasted away some granite and uncovered a small cavern hidden in solid rock. In the cave on a tiny ledge, cross-legged, with his hands folded in his lap, sat a wee mummified man no more than fourteen inches tall. Naturally, the miners were astonished.

X rays and other scientific studies showed that he had a completely human skeleton. His teeth were intact, and he had apparently been about sixty-five years old at the time of his death. But no one could even guess when he had lived or died.

Pottery, tools and dried food have provided clues to the age of many ancient tombs, but no bowls, trays of food or tools of stone had been placed in the cave tomb with the tiny mummified man.

Since we lack any clues as to when this strange small fellow had lived and have nothing to tell us whether he was an ordinary mortal or was considered a rarity even in his own time, he remains to this day a mystery.

One writer familiar with the small, fine-boned, golden-skinned bushmen of South Africa wonders whether they may have lived in northern lands in the pre-glacial era and fled southward before the advancing cold and glaciers of the last Ice Age. Could they be the basis for the tales of small, clever brownies who are willing to be helpful to people who treat them well as long as the brownies can remain safely out of sight?

There are of course occasional individuals who are dwarfed by some imbalance in the glands, a disorder in the bones or other genetic quirk. Midgets are born by chance to normal-sized parents. In olden days parents to whom such a child was born might well have thought that a fairy changeling child had been given to them.

But some reports of "little people" of a lost day and age are more mysterious than these.

Stranded Space Travelers?

A full grown man fourteen inches tall is as odd in his way as the skeletons found in 1938 in the mountain caves of southern China. In rows of small graves were small skeletons with slender bones but large skulls. There were rock drawings in the same caves showing the sun, moon and planets and depicting figures wearing round helmets. And hundreds of flat round plates of granite with strange writing on them were found at the site.

It is said that this writing, when it was deciphered, told of an aircraft that crashed on the earth about 12,000 years ago. Where it had come from was not clear. The crew had no materials with which to repair their craft or build a new one in which to escape. They tried to make friends with the people who lived in the mountains but did not succeed. So they hid in the caves, where, it appears, they were hunted down and killed. Amazingly, in the legends of the mountain people there is a tale of some small, thin beings who came down from the clouds and were killed because they were so very ugly.

Others who read about these small skeletons and the other-worldly story connected with them are reminded of reports of landings of unidentified flying objects (see pp. 91–98.) For in the few cases in which crews of spaceships have been sighted, they have all been described as small and wearing slight round helmets on their heads.

EPILOGUE

In Pursuit of the Unknown

Will they ever be solved, these mysteries of the strange peoples who have vanished from the earth, or those who perhaps inhabit some distant planet we cannot even see as a dot of light in the evening sky?

Men's curious minds are delving ever deeper into the past and into the universe. It is certain that the future will unlock some of the hidden secrets of time and space. Since patient research has brought legends like that of the Trojan War into the realm of verified history, it may be that the riddle of Atlantis will also be solved. Links may be found to the giants and midgets whose branches seem to have broken away from the family tree of man. And communication may be established with beings on other worlds.

Mysterious creatures of the seas may be trapped in the nets or speared by the harpoons of men. Or perhaps new understanding of the oceans will show that the legends of the ages have been much more than inventive fantasies.

Explorers are at work and will very likely succeed in probing the mysteries of the human mind. Perhaps the mental powers that today seem eerie and inexplicable, fanciful and elusive, will someday be comprehended, measured and controlled. Whether as human beings we shall be richer or poorer for that understanding remains to be seen. Indeed, the uses that will be made of our future discoveries and the ways they may affect the lives of those who come after us combine to form the infinitely fascinating mystery of the future.

For whatever inroads are made into the unknown, there will always be uncharted territory. Even as the wide range of phenomena we class today as mysteries is swept bare of shielding clouds by man's relentless passion to know, we may be confident that beyond them still wider horizons will loom, clouded with even grander mysteries.

Index

A

Abominable Snowmen, 15
Alchemy, 110–112
Alexander, Rolf, 72
America, monsters of, 17, 20
American Indians
  and Atlantis, 130
  Croatans, 129
  and rainmaking, 72–73
Aristotle, 110, 112
Astral being, 27, 52, 54
  and auras, 76
  doppelgänger, 53
  of plants, 82
  and silver cord, 54
Astral projection, 54, 55, 57; *see also* Astral travel
Astral travel, 53–55
  experiment in, 55
  and lamas, 57
  learning, 54
  and Sherman, General, 53–54
Astrology, 113–115
Atlantis, 121, 130–131, 132, 140
  and Amerindians, 130
  and Cayce, Edgar, 131
  and Great Flood, 131
  and Minoans, 131
  and Plato, 130
  and Santorini, 131
Aura(s), 74–76, 82
  "clouds of glory," 75
  colors of, 75–76
  definitions of, 74–75
  diagnosing disease, 76, 82
  disappearance of, 76
  interpretations of, 76
  Kirlian photography of, 74, 75, 76
  of plants, 82
  religious, 75, 76
  seeing your own, 76
Australopithecus, 136
Automatic writing, 39, 42, 46–47
  ouija board, 47–48

B

Bermuda triangle, 128
Bigfoot, 16–17
Black Mass, 105
Black Sabbath, 102, 103, 105
Blimp, abandoned, 127
Boleyn, Anne, 49
Brain waves, 31, 32
  and astral projection, 55
Brownies, 137, 138

C

Caldwell, Taylor
  and automatic writing, 46
  and reincarnation, 62, 63–64
Cards, fortunetelling, 108, 123–124
Catalepsy, 29
Cayce, Edgar, 85–86, 131
Changelings, 137, 138
Charms
  love, 109
  magic, 106
  sorcerers', 109
  See also talismans
Clairaudience, 36–37
Clairsentience, 37
Clairvoyance, 36–38
  and auras, 74, 76
  psychometry, 38
  reading crystal, 120
Cleidomancy, 122
"Clouds of glory," 75
Coffee grounds, for fortunetelling, 124
"Control," 43
Covens, 102
Crete, and Atlantis, 131
Croatans, and Roanoke, 129
Crystal balls, 120
Crystal skull, 120–121

D

Dare, Virginia, 129
Dead, contact with, *see* Spirits; Spiritualism
Death spells, 109
Déjà vu, 58, 60
Delphic Oracle, 108
Demon-worship, 20, 106; *see also* Witchcraft
Dervishes, 30
Diagnosing disease
  auras, 76
  Cayce, Edgar, 85–86
  plants, 82
Dickens, Charles, 46
Disappearances, mysterious, 125–132
  Atlantis, 130–131, 132, 140
  and Bermuda triangle, 128
  blimp, abandoned, 127
  civilizations, lost, 130–132
  of Eskimos 129
  of giants, 133–136
  Lemuria, 132
  of little people, 137–138
  Marie Celeste, 126–127
  of Minoans, 131
  of peoples of past, 133–139
  Roanoke, 129
  Seabird, 126
  settlements, lost, 129
  ships, abandoned, 126–127
  of Viking colonies, 129
Diviners, *see* Sorcerers
Divining rods, 71
Doppelgänger, 53
Dowsing, 70–71
Doyle, Sir Arthur Conan, 45
Dwarfs, 137, 138

E

Easter Island, 134
Elasmosaurs, 11
Endor, woman of, 101
Energy
  of crystal skull, 121
  fields, 80–81
  magnetic, 71, 120, 122
  universal, 113
Eskimos
  disappearance of, 129
  and reincarnation, 64
Exorcism, 51, 105
Extrasensory perception, 31, 32–38
  and brain waves, 31, 32
  clairaudience, 36–37
  claisentience, 37
  clairvoyance, 36–38
  in East, 40–41
  experiments in, 31, 32–35
  psychometry, 38
  See also Telepathy

F

Fairies, 137, 138
Faith healing, 85, 86–89
Fakirs, 30
"Familiar," 101, 102
Flames, strange, 90
"Flying saucers," 97; *see also* Unidentified flying objects
Forecasting future, 100, 107–108, 120–121; *see also* Fortunetelling
Foreknowledge, 58–59
  déjà vu, 58, 59
  precognition, 58, 59
  premonitions, 59
  "wrinkle in time" theory, 59
Fortunetelling, 99, 113–124

astrology, 113–115
cards, 108, 123–124
cleidomancy, 122
coffee grounds, 124
crystal balls, 120
crystal skull, 120–121
Delphic Oracle, 108
handwriting analysis, 118
horoscopes, 113
"magic eye," 122
Magic Nine, 124
palmistry, 116–117
phrenology, 118–119
by sorcerers, 107–108
tarot cards, 108, 123–124
tea leaves, 124
"Four-not-likes," 13
Fox, Kate and Margaret, 42
Free association, 27
Freud, Sigmund, 27

G

Gateway of the Sun, 134
Ghosts, 49–52
Giants, 133–136
Glenn, John, and UFOs, 93–94
Graphology, 118
Great Flood, and Atlantis, 131

H

Hammurabi, King, 101
Hand of Glory, 109
Handwriting analysis, 118
Harz Mountains, witchcraft in, 102
Hatfield, Charles, 72
Healing, 85–89
Hex marks, 105
Hibernation, 68–69
Himalayas, monsters, of, 15, 17
Home, Daniel Douglas, 57
Homing instinct, 77–78
Horoscopes, 113
Hypertrichosis, 19
Hypnosis, 26–30
  in Africa, 30
  catalepsy, 29
  and dervishes, 30
  and fakirs, 30
  and levitation, 56
  mass, 29
  past lives, uncovering, 28
  post-hypnotic suggestion, 26
  and prenatal recall, 27
  and reincarnation, 60, 62, 132
  self-, 28–29, 30, 43
  and snake charming, 84
  as therapy, 27
  and yoga, 28–29, 30, 32

J

Jack-o-lanterns, 102–103

K

Karma, 60
Kirlian photography, 74, 75, 76
"Kiss of Death," 84
Krakatoa, clairvoyance and, 36–37

L

Lamas
  and astral projection, 57
  and astral travel, 53
  and auras, 75
  and levitation, 57
  psychics, 40
Lemuria, 132
Leprechauns, 137
Levitation, 56–57
"Lie detectors," and plants, 81–82
Little people, 137–138, 140
Loch Ness monster, 24
Lorelei, 21
Lost civilizations, 130–132, 140
Lost settlements, 129
Lourdes, 88–89
Love charms, 109
Lycanthropy, 19, 20

M

Magic
  in alchemy, 112
  black, 99, 100
  charms, 106
  pentacles, 109
Magic Candle, 109
"Magic eye," 122
Magic Nine, 124
Marie Celeste, 126–127
Mass hypnosis, 29
Medicine men, 40, 105–106
Medium(s)
  and "control," 43
  fake, 42
  Fox, Kate and Margaret, 42
  Home, Daniel Douglas, 57
  intermediaries, 102
  and trances, 43, 45, 46
  and Worth, Patience, 48
Merlin, 100
Mermaids, 21–23
Merman, 23
Midgets, 138, 140
Midsummer's Eve, 102, 109
Minoans, and Atlantis, 131
Monsters, 10–24
  Abominable Snowmen, 15
  American, 17
  Bigfoot, 16–17
  Himalayan, 15, 17
  lake-dwelling, 24
  Loch Ness, 24
  mermaids, 21–23
  pre-human, 15–17
  sea serpents, 11
  sirens, 21
  Susquatch, 16–17
  vampires, 20
  werewolves, 18–20
  yeti, 15, 17
Mummy, midget, 138
Murphy, Bridey, 28
Mystery, definition of, 8
The Mystery of Edwin Drood
  Dickens, 46

N

Necromancy, 102, 112
Nimbus, 75
Nirvana, 60

O

Occult, 99–124
  alchemy, 110–112
  fortunetelling, 99, 113–124
  sorcery, 99, 107–109
  witchcraft, 99, 100–106
Oracle
  crystal skull, 120–121
  Delphic, 108
Ouija board, 47–48

P

Palmistry, 116–117
Parapsychology
  auras, research in, 75
  definition of, 40
  experiments in, 31
Pentacles, 109
Philosopher's stone, 112
Philters, sorcerers', 109
Photography
  Kirlian, of auras, 74, 75, 76
  of Loch Ness monster, 24
  of plant auras, 82
  of spirits, 45
Phrenology, 118–119
Pillars of Hercules, 130
Pixies, 137
Plants, 79–82
  auras of, 82
  diagnosing ailments, 82
  energy fields of, 80–81
  experiments with, 79–82
  feelings in, 79–82

polygraphs, testing with, 81–82
prayed-over, 79–80
response to music, 79
response to people, 79, 82
response to psychic suggestion, 79
Plato, and Atlantis, 130
Plesiosaurs, 11
Poltergeists, 50–51, 52
Polygraphs, and plants, 81–82
Porphyria, 19
Post-hypnotic suggestion, 26
Potions
   love, 109
   protective, 109
   unicorn horn, 13
   witches', 105
Prana, 30
Precognition, 58, 59
Prehistoric structures, 134–135
Pre-humans, 15–17, 136
Premonitions, 59
Prenatal recall, 27
"Psi force," 35
Psychic phenomena
   abandoned ships, 126–127
   alchemy, 110–112
   astral projection, 54, 55, 57
   astral travel, 53–55
   astrology, 113–115
   Atlantis, 121, 130–131, 132, 140
   auras, 74–76, 82
   automatic writing, 39, 42, 46–47
   Bermuda triangle, 128
   disappearances, mysterious, 125–132
   dowsing, 71–72
   Eastern, 40–41
   energy, psychic, 51, 52, 80–81, 113, 120, 121, 122
   extrasensory perception, 31, 32–38
   flames, strange, 90
   foreknowledge, 58–59
   fortunetelling, 99, 113–124
   ghosts, 49–52
   healing, 85–89
   hibernation, 68–69
   homing instinct, 77–78
   hypnosis, 26–30
   levitation, 56–57
   lost civilizations, 130–132
   lost settlements, 129
   occult, 99–124
   ouija board, 47–48
   and parapsychology, 31, 40, 75
   in plants, 79–82
   prana, 30
   psychokinesis, 52
   rainmaking, 72–73
   reincarnation, 60–64
   skin sight, 66–67
   snake charming, 83–84
   sorcery, 99, 107–109
   spirits, contacts with, 39, 42–52
   spiritualism, 42–52
   telepathy, 32–33
   thought transfer, 31–35
   unidentified flying objects, 91–98, 139
   vanished peoples, 133–139
   witchcraft, 99, 100–106
   "wrinkle in time" theory, 59
Psychics
   African, 40
   and astral travel, 53, 54
   and auras, 74, 75
   Caldwell, Taylor, 46, 62, 63–64
   Cayce, Edgar, 85–86, 131
   Eastern, 40–41, 53, 56–57, 60, 61–62
   Fox, Kate and Margaret, 42
   healers, 74, 75, 85–87
   Home, Daniel Douglas, 57
   and levitation, 57
   mediums, 39, 42, 43–45, 46, 48, 57, 102
   and plants, 79
   Strindberg, August, 62–63
   Worrall, Ambrose and Olga, 86
Psychoanalysis, 27
Psychokinesis, 52
Psychometry, 38

R

Rainmaking, 72–73
   Alexander, Rolf, 72
   and American Indians, 72–73
   Hatfield, Charles, 72
Ramayana, and UFOs, 95–96
Reincarnation, 28, 60–64, 132
   African, 64
   and Atlantis, 132
   Buddhist, 60
   and Caldwell, Taylor, 62, 63–64
   Eskimo, 64
   and geniuses, 64
   Greek, 60
   Hindu, 60
   in India, 60, 61–62
   karma, 60
   and Lemuria, 132
   and literature, 62–64
   of Murphy, Bridey, 28
   nirvana, 60
   and Strindberg, August, 62–63
   trace recollections, 60, 62–64, 132
Roanoke, 129

S

Salem witch trials, 105
Santorini, and Atlantis, 131
Sea serpents, 11
Seabird, 126
Seances, 42–45, 57
   accounts of, 43, 45, 57
   automatic writing at, 42
   and "control," 43
   fake, 42
   "spirit circles," 42
   table tapping at, 42, 43
   table tilting at 42, 43
   techniques of, 42
Self-hypnosis, 28–29, 30, 43
Sherman, General, and astral travel, 53–54
Ships, abandoned, 126–127
   blimp, 127
   Marie Celeste, 126–127
   Seabird, 126
Silver cord, 54
Sirens, 21
Skin sight, 66–67
Sleepwalking, 54
Snake charmer, 83–84
Solon, and Atlantis, 130
Sorcerers, 100, 107–109
   Delphic Oracle, 108
   forecasting future, 107, 108
   invisible, 109
   in Middle Ages, 105, 107
   talismans of, 105, 107, 109
   See also Sorcery
Sorcery, 99, 107–109
   Black Sabbath, 102
   forecasting future, 107–108
   Hand of Glory, 109
   invisibility, 109
   love charms, 109
   Magic Candle, 109
   pentacles, 109
   philters, 109
   sors, 107
   spells, 109
   See also Sorcerers
Soubirous, Bernadette, 88
Space travel, hibernation and, 68, 69
Space travelers, 97–98
   and giants, 133
   small, 139
Spaceships, *see* Unidentified flying objects
Spells, 100, 109
Spirit being, 27
   and auras, 76
   See also Astral being
"Spirit Circles," 42
Spirits
   Boleyn, Anne, 49
   contacts with, 39, 42–52, 102
   "control," 43
   Dickens, Charles, 46
   Doyle, Sir Arthur Conan, 45
   ghosts, 49–52

and literature, 46, 48
necromancy, 102
poltergeists, 50–51, 52
at seances, 45
Worth, Patience, 48
Spiritualism, 42–52
automatic writing, 39, 42, 46–47
"control," 43
Fox, Kate and Margaret, 42
ghosts, 49–52
levitation, 56–57
mediums, 39, 42, 43–45, 46, 48, 57, 102
ouija board, 47–48
poltergeists, 50–51, 52
seances, 42, 43–45, 57
"spirit circles," 42
Strindberg, August, and reincarnation, 62–63
Stubbs, Peter, 19
Sun signs, 113–115
Susquatch, 16–17

T

Table tapping, 42, 43
Table tilting, 42, 43
Talismans
forecasting future, 107
Hand of Glory, 109
sorcerers', 105, 107, 109
witches', 105
Tarot cards, 108, 123–124
Tea leaves, for fortunetelling, 124
Telepathy, 32–35
and animals, 34
electromagnetic waves and, 34–35
experiments in, 32–35
and "psi force," 35
Thought transfer, 31–35
in Africa, 40
and brain waves, 31, 32
clairaudience, 36–37
clairsentience, 37
clairvoyance, 36–38
in East, 40–41
experiments in, 31, 32–35
extrasensory perception, 31, 32–38
psychometry, 38
telepathy, 32–35
Titanic, clairvoyance and, 36
Trance
and astral travel, 54
and automatic writing, 46
and Caldwell, Taylor, 62, 63–64
catalepsy, 29
of Delphic Oracle, 108
hypnotic, 26–30, 43, 56, 60, 62
and levitation, 56, 57
and reincarnation, 60, 62–64

sleep healing, 85–86
sleepwalking, 54
speaking from, 42, 43
yoga, 28–29, 30
Travel
astral, 53–55
and homing instinct, 77–78
space, 68, 69

U

Unicorn, 12–14
Unidentified flying objects, 91–98, 139
ancient, 95–96
astronauts' and cosmonauts' sightings of, 93–94
in Bible, 96
explained, 91
Glenn, John, report of, 93–94
landings of, 97, 139
and little people, 139
older sightings, 92, 93
radio messages from, 98
recent sightings, 91, 92–94, 97
travelers in, 97–98, 139

V

Vampirism, 20
Viking colonies, disappearance of, 129

W

Warlocks, 100, 105, *see also* Witches, Witchcraft
"Water witches," 71
Werewolves, 18–20
Wilde, Oscar, 46
Witch(es), 99, 100–106
covens, 102
doctors, 105–106
Endor, woman of, 101
evil, 100
executions of, 105
"familiar" of, 101, 102
flying, 103
good, 100
hunts, 105
medicine men, 105–106
in Middle Ages, 103, 105
modern, 105–106
potions of, 105
protection against, 105
in Salem, Massachusetts, 105
Shakespearean, 99
sorcerers, 100
talismans of, 105
warlocks, 100, 105
See also Witchcraft

Witchcraft, 99, 100–106
ancient, 101
Black Mass, 105
Black Sabbath, 102, 103, 105
evil-doing, 100
Halloween, 102
and Hammurabi, King, 101
in Harz Mountains, 102
jack-o-lanterns, 102–103
Midsummer's Eve, 102
modern, 105–106
See also Witch(es)
Witches' Sabbath, 102, 103, 105
Wizard rods, 71
Wizards, 99, 100
Merlin, 100
Woman of Endor, 101
Worrall, Ambrose and Olga, 86
Worth Patience, 48
"Wrinkle in time" theory, 59

Y

Yeti, 15, 17
Yoga, 28–29, 30, 32
and levitation, 56–57
Yogis, 28–29, 30
and levitation, 56–57
psychics, 40–41

Z

Zodiac, signs of, 113–115